THINKERTHINGS

A Student-generated Approach to Language Experience

Sharon Miller
Wallace Judd

A Addison-Wesley Publishing Company

Menlo Park, California · Reading, Massachussetts

London · Amsterdam · Don Mills, Ontario · Sydney

Sharron Miller is a teacher and assistant principal at Carmel River School in Carmel, California.

Wallace Judd has been a teacher at Brentwood and Runnymede Schools, East Palo Alto, California, at Carmel River School, Carmel, California, and at Bayside Middle School, San Mateo, California.

This book is published by the Addison-Wesley Innovative Division.

ISBN-0-201-03453-0

BCDEFGHIJK—EB—83210

Contents

Introduction

ThinkerThings are worksheets designed to provide interesting language experiences for students in the intermediate grades (4-8). The front of each worksheet is designed to be duplicated by photocopying or by making a duplicator master with a Thermofax machine. The back of each worksheet shows answers.

ThinkerThings is a sneak attack on language skills—in much the same way as an entertaining TV commercial is a disguised attack on the viewer's sales resistance. By playing games, making up problems for other students, and generally having a good time with words, students have a chance to explore and master language as no amount of drill would do.

The concept of student-generated activities

Each page ends with an extension, an invitation to the student to create problems similar to those on the page. These extensions lead to student-generated curriculum, worksheets made up from the students' own problems. It is vitally important that these be shared with the entire class, either in verbal or duplicator master form, to reinforce the students' efforts. This process allows the students to become creators of the curriculum, rather than passive observers, or at best, the ones acted on by the curriculum. The difference is crucial.

Sequencing

The activities within each unit are sequenced from easier to more difficult. For example, in the unit on classifying, the opening activities on "Crosses" and "Categories" are easier and more motivational than the activities at the end of the unit on "Want Ads" and the "Telephone Book."

The units, however, can be done in any order. So, if you are working on comprehension and context at the beginning of the year, feel free to use the materials in that unit to support your teaching, even though the unit is placed sixth in **ThinkerThings**.

Time allotments

Needless to say, the pages take varying amounts of class time, depending on the abilities of the students. Normally, they will take fifteen to twenty minutes, with the all-important student generation of examples taking another ten or fifteen.

If you can't schedule that much time in a period for using **Thinker Things**, assign the student-generated part as homework. If you would like to use the entire period, allow the students to trade activities and work each others'. They'll enjoy it, and so will you.

A unit on any skill could take as little as three or four days to complete; or it might take as much as two to three weeks, depending on the amount of time each day devoted to these activities.

Examples

The examples are placed anywhere on the page so that the student is encouraged to look over the whole page before beginning. This strategy introduces students to the idea of skipping difficult problems and coming back to them after they've done some of the easier ones. They see the page as a whole, rather than as tied in to a predetermined sequence.

Level of difficulty

According to the Dale-Chall reading formula, the average grade level of **Thinker Things** is 5.7. Of course, individual worksheets vary considerably in reading level, depending on their nature. In the feature of this teachers' manual called "Using the Page", you will find suggestions as to how to make the activity easier or more difficult, depending on the abilities of your students.

Send us your examples

All these pages have been used with a variety of students at many different grade levels. The responses of both students and teachers have been positive, engaging, and have led the authors to assemble the pages into a book.

If you and your class create some examples that you really like, please send them to us in care of the Innovative Division, Addison-Wesley Publishing Company, Menlo Park, California 94025. With your permission, and giving credit to you and your students, we would like to make up another collection of **Thinker Things.**

Index of skills

Comprehension ───────────

Research skills ───────────

Index of skills, chart form

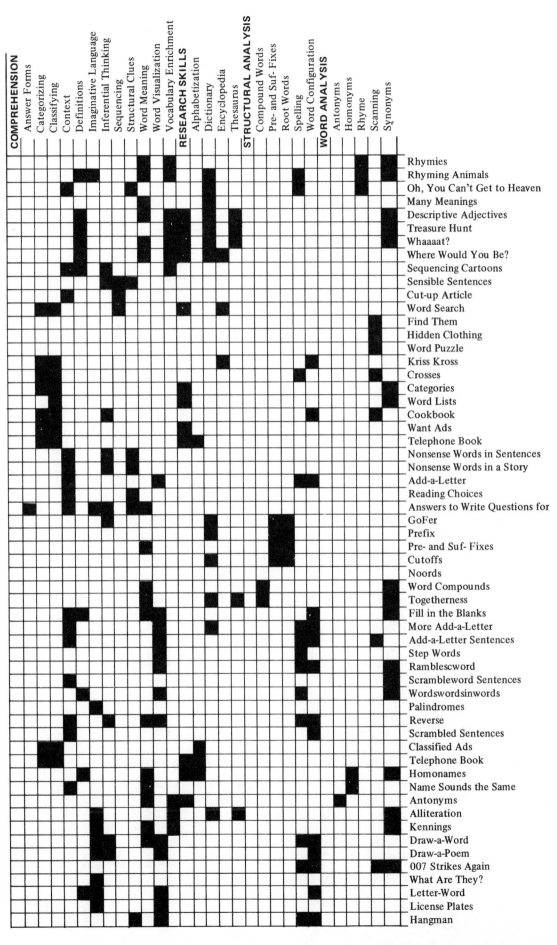

Column headings:

COMPREHENSION — Answer Forms, Categorizing, Classifying, Context, Definitions, Imaginative Language, Inferential Thinking, Sequencing, Structural Clues, Word Meaning, Word Visualization, Vocabulary Enrichment

RESEARCH SKILLS — Alphabetization, Dictionary, Encyclopedia, Thesaurus

STRUCTURAL ANALYSIS — Compound Words, Pre- and Suf- Fixes, Root Words, Spelling, Word Configuration

WORD ANALYSIS — Antonyms, Homonyms, Rhyme, Scanning, Synonyms

Row labels:

- Rhymies
- Rhyming Animals
- Oh, You Can't Get to Heaven
- Many Meanings
- Descriptive Adjectives
- Treasure Hunt
- Whaaaat?
- Where Would You Be?
- Sequencing Cartoons
- Sensible Sentences
- Cut-up Article
- Word Search
- Find Them
- Hidden Clothing
- Word Puzzle
- Kriss Kross
- Crosses
- Categories
- Word Lists
- Cookbook
- Want Ads
- Telephone Book
- Nonsense Words in Sentences
- Nonsense Words in a Story
- Add-a-Letter
- Reading Choices
- Answers to Write Questions for
- GoFer
- Prefix
- Pre- and Suf- Fixes
- Cutoffs
- Noords
- Word Compounds
- Togetherness
- Fill in the Blanks
- More Add-a-Letter
- Add-a-Letter Sentences
- Step Words
- Ramblescword
- Scrambleword Sentences
- Wordswordsinwords
- Palindromes
- Reverse
- Scrambled Sentences
- Classified Ads
- Telephone Book
- Homonames
- Name Sounds the Same
- Antonyms
- Alliteration
- Kennings
- Draw-a-Word
- Draw-a-Poem
- 007 Strikes Again
- What Are They?
- Letter-Word
- License Plates
- Hangman

Rhyming activities

Rhymies are a good, lively way to start things off. More than just fun, these exercises teach students how to search for synonyms and to devise some sort of strategy for solving rhymies.

Rhyming Animals build on the experience the student has gained in doing the rhymies. In these exercises the student has to select what he thinks is the obvious half of the answer, and work from it to the other, more obscure rhymed word.

"Oh, You Can't Get to Heaven" is an old camp song that the children don't have to sing to enjoy. As they make up verses, they not only have to rhyme, but they develop some sense of poetic meter and general stanza form. At first, they may need a lot of "poetic license," but their later attempts will probably reward you well.

Rhymies ———————————————————— DUPLICATOR 1

Objectives
> finding synonyms for a word
> making rhymes
> using the dictionary and thesaurus
> vocabulary enrichment
> recognition and enjoyment of word patterns

Using the Page
1. Play as an oral guessing game first.
2. Make up small groups that brainstorm rhymies.
3. Correct the worksheet orally, and share ones the students think up.
4. Use names of students in your class for some, e.g., "angry James" is "frowning Browning"; "scarlet Mendoza" is "red Ted"; "trap Buser" is "snare Claire".

Creating Their Own
> The easiest way to generate rhymies is to make up the rhyming pair first, then find synonyms for the two words. Encourage your students to use the dictionary or thesaurus to find interesting words to use in the definition. Be sure you have some way of sharing what the children have written. Make up another duplicator master with their examples, put their rhymies on flash cards, do a rhymie bulletin board, or play an oral guessing game with them.

Additional rhymies

tidy toes	neat feat
stupid hobo	dumb bum
delayed blackbird	slow crow
liberated elm	free tree

Rhyming Animals ———————————————————— DUPLICATOR 2

Objectives

using context clues to figure out a word
finding synonyms
using rhyme—finding similar vowel sounds
vocabulary enrichment

Using the Page

1. To make it easier, write definitions under some of the blanks. "We_____the_____ singing behind the fence." (listened to) (feathered flyer)

2. Give a clue before the sentence. "What sings besides you?" might be a clue to the sentence above.

3. Make up a set of cards to go with the page. Each card would have one answer written on it. The student could find one word that fits and then search for an appropriate rhyme.

Creating Their Own

The student must zero in on a clue in the sentence that will give him one of the missing words with a fair degree of certainty. Then he can try other words in the second blank that might fit.

In making up sentences of this type, students should be cautioned against sentences that are too general, that don't give specific enough clues to key one of the words.

Additional Rhyming Animals

luck duck	beaver weaver
horse course	shark mark dark
take snake	squirrel curl girl
crow slow	third bird heard
fat bat	bear tear hair
goat coat	jay play way

"Oh, You Can't Get to Heaven" ———————————————— DUPLICATOR 3

Objectives

reasoning to produce rhymes
creating poetic lines

Using the Page

1. Sing the verses after the students have completed them.

2. Record different verses that the students have made up. Stop the recorder and see if the students can finish the verse.

3. Split the class in half. Have one half make up the first line, then ask the second to finish it. If they can't, the first side has to finish the verse. Switch.

Creating Their Own

Start with the easy part of making up some funny way somebody might try to get to heaven. "Oh, you can't get to Heaven *by singing a tune."* Then ask the students to name a few words that rhyme with *tune*, and that relate to singing. They might say *croon* or *soon* or something. See if these rhymes give them any clue. If they hit a dead end, tell them to try *song* instead of *tune*, and keep trying. The entire exercise should encourage inventiveness and foster outlandish modes of travel as well as fantasy objections.

Additional Verses

1.   . . . in a big white cloud,
   'cause floating up there is not allowed.

2.   . . . by lying in bed,
   'cause you'll go the other way when you are dead.

3.   . . . on a pogo stick,
   'cause the bounce and jounce will make you sick.

Word meaning

Many Meanings explores the fact that many words have more than one meaning. The child must find a word that has both of the given meanings.

Descriptive Adjectives is designed to teach what adjectives are and to encourage the children to use the dictionary to find out the meanings of the adjectives and list people whom they describe.

Treasure Hunt is a set of whimsical sentences with at least one word in each sentence which the child must look up in the dictionary in order to answer the questions.

Whaaaat? is a group of outrageous sentences with difficult words in them. The child must look the words up in the dictionary and translate the sentences into everyday language.

Where Would You Be? is a set of questions involving exotic dress and sites. The children must use the dictionary to see where they would be.

Dictionary work can be dull, and it is hoped that presenting new vocabulary in these different ways will motivate your children to want to find words and their meanings.

Many Meanings ————————————————— DUPLICATOR 4

Objectives
> using the dictionary
> vocabulary enrichment
> exploring multiple meanings of words

Using the Page
1. Do some orally first.
2. Look around the classroom and find things that have more than one meaning (face, clock, board, book, etc.).
3. Have the children complete the worksheet and share orally ones they have created.
4. Make a worksheet on which the children can draw more than one meaning for a word. Use such words as play, run, roll, race, top, etc.
5. To make the worksheet easier, the answers could be scrambled at the bottom of the page.

Creating Their Own

Have the students find words which have multiple meanings in the dictionary. They should try to find words familiar to other children. They then list two of the definitions for others to solve. These can be shared orally or you can make up a worksheet of the ones the children created.

Additional Examples

1. run—hole in stocking; race
2. king—monarch; chess piece
3. ring—something you wear on your finger; to resound
4. needle—a pin with a hole; pine tree leaf
5. bark—dog noise; tree trunk covering
6. tie—to knot; neck piece

Descriptive Adjectives ——————————————————— DUPLICATOR 5

Objectives

using the dictionary
using the thesaurus
learning to use synonyms
learning adjectives

Using the Page

1. Do some oral examples, using simple adjectives.

2. Correct the worksheet orally together.

3. Have the children list adjectives that describe animals, or other nouns, and make a worksheet using their suggestions.

4. Share the ones the children have created, either orally or by making another worksheet.

Creating Their Own

The children should think of simple adjectives which describe people (or other nouns). Then, by using the dictionary or thesaurus, have them find more difficult synonyms for their adjectives. These more difficult words are the ones to use on the worksheet or orally.

Additional Examples

affectionate, patient, placid, tow-headed

Treasure Hunt ——————————————————— DUPLICATOR 6

Objectives

using the dictionary and thesaurus
vocabulary enrichment
finding synonyms

Using the Page

1. Distribute the worksheet and do the first one together, if necessary.

2. When the children have completed the worksheet, make a master of the ones they create.

Creating Their Own

Have the children write a simple sentence. Then, using the dictionary or thesaurus, they should replace one of the words with a more difficult synonym.

Another possibility is to have them thumb through the dictionary and find a difficult word which is interesting to them. Then they can use their new word in a sentence.

Additional Examples

1. Who wears monocles?
2. If you invited an aardvark to tea, what would you serve?
3. What is your favorite kind of torte?
4. If you saw a sidewinder approaching, where would you be?
5. Where would you see a cumulus formation?

WHAAAAT? —————————————————————————— DUPLICATOR 7

Objectives

using the dictionary
vocabulary enrichment
using synonyms

Using the Page

1. Do the first one together orally.

2. Have children complete the worksheet and correct it orally.

3. To make the worksheet easier, you may want to list the answers at the bottom of the page.

4. Make a worksheet of the sentences the children create, or do them together on the chalkboard.

Creating Their Own

Ask the students to write a simple sentence. Using the dictionary or thesaurus, have them find synonyms for some of the words in the sentence and rewrite them, using the more difficult words.

Additional Examples

1. Gloom descended upon the gladiators subsequent to their defeat.
2. The skunk emitted a noxious odor.
3. The simian leaped around mirthfully.
4. Youngsters desire delectable dishes.
5. Travail is the antithesis of play.

Where Would You Be? —————————————————————— DUPLICATOR 8

Objectives

using the dictionary
using the encyclopedia
vocabulary enrichment

Using the Page

1. Do the first one together orally.

2. Have the children complete the worksheet. You may want to correct them orally together.

3. Play a game in which you find the locations on a map.

Creating Their Own

Have the children sit down with an encyclopedia or dictionary, looking for buildings, clothing, animals, or other objects characteristic of a foreign country or continent. Then have each write a sentence asking where someone would be if he were to see that object.

Additional Examples

1. Where would you be if you saw: the Great Wall? a macaw? a road runner?

2. Where would you be if you had on: knickers; an ascot; a slicker; clogs; mufti?

Sequencing

Sequencing Cartoons is an interesting way to provide sequencing practice for children. The cartoon frames are cut out and assembled in correct order by the children.

Sensible Sentences are goofy scrambled sentences which the children must arrange correctly to make sense.

Cut-up Article is a series of paragraphs from a newspaper article or old book which the children cut up and reassemble in the proper order.

These activities can add some humor and motivation to the teaching of sequencing.

Sequencing Cartoons ───────────────────────────── DUPLICATOR 9

Objectives
> sequencing
> context clues
> inferential thinking

Using the Page
1. Discuss cartoons, humor, and how important order is to evoking humor.
2. Discuss the solution of the cartoon sequence with the students.
3. Ask the children to cut cartoons out of the newspaper and mount them on cards or heavy paper and shuffle the frames. Comic strips out of the Sunday paper with ten or twelve frames are much more difficult than the normal three or four found in the daily strip. Unnecessary frames can be omitted.
4. You can duplicate a cartoon that has been cut up, so the students can cut it out and tape it together in the proper order.
5. For a little variety, the children might color the cartoons when they've ordered them.

Creating Their Own
Repeat (3) above. This time, have the children mount the frames on separate 3″ x 5″ cards or on tagboard cards. You may want to laminate the cards with clear contact paper. By doing this you will have thirty sequencing activities for an interest center or for the children to exchange and arrange.

The children may wish to create original comic strips. Encourage this by copying their work and distributing it to the other children.

Objectives

sequencing skills

grammatical clues to structure

Using the Page

1.   Write a scrambled sentence on the chalkboard and ask the students to rearrange the words so they make sense.

2.   Make up a similar worksheet, incorporating the names of some of the children in your class into the sentences.

3.   Correct the worksheet together orally.

4.   For easier worksheets, make the sentences shorter. Longer ones make the work more difficult.

Creating Their Own

Have the children write sentences, then scramble the words. Make a worksheet of their sentences or do them on the blackboard.

Additional Examples

1.   the Ivan tiny mice Terrible tasted the

2.   during the ferociously sea hurricane the churned frightening

3.   if split ache experience is a afterward don't you banana a stomach eating delightful a (burp!) get

Regarding the answers provided, actually, any sequence that is sensible is correct. Encourage the children to come up with more than one correct solution.

Objectives

sequencing skills

context clues

Using the Page

1.   Have the children cut out the article and reassemble it in order. Discuss the solution orally.

2.   Cut articles out of children's periodicals, old books, or the newspaper. Cut the paragraphs apart and mount each one on a separate card.

Creating Their Own

Have the children cut out articles and exchange the pieces of their articles with other students. Make sure they check their own article for paragraphs that could be omitted, or that could be inserted in the article at different places.

The children may want to write original articles that can be cut up into paragraphs for sequencing.

Incidentally, these paragraphs describe an actual tightrope walk make by Philippe Petit between the two towers of the World Trade Center, 1350 feet above the streets of New York.

Scanning

Word Search is a puzzle form of a scanning activity. Topical words are hidden in a letter grid and the student must find them.

Find Them is a scanning activity where children's names are hidden in sentences and the student must find and circle them.

Hidden Clothing is a variation of "Find Them" involving articles of clothing.

Word Puzzle is a scanning activity where the student reads the entire sentence to solve it. The words are divided in irregular places, and the child puts the letters together to form words and a sensible sentence.

Kriss Kross is a form of crossword puzzle with the answers at the bottom of the page. The student completes the puzzle by putting the proper words in the blanks.

Word Search ———————————————————————— DUPLICATOR 12

Objectives

> scanning
> categorizing
> research skills

Using the Page

1. Explain to the children how to find the words. They can move one space at a time in any direction, up, down, sideways, or diagonally.
2. Create a word search yourself using the names of the students in your class. (Be sure to include all of them.)
3. To make an easier word search for younger children, make all the words go from left to right, and make the word search smaller.
4. To make a more difficult word search, make it larger.
5. Make a large word search on butcher paper. Put it on the bulletin board, and have the children find and circle the answers.

Creating Their Own

> Have the children select topics interesting to them. Football teams, animals, last names, math words, are all possible subjects. They then go to some resource such as the encyclopedia, almanac, or library book to make a list.

Using a piece of graph paper and a pencil, have the students write their words at random. When all the words are located on the grid, have them fill in the blanks with any letters they choose. Make a duplicator master of the grid and distribute copies to the class. Be certain each student signs his puzzle.

Additional Topics
sports, plants, flowers, colors, clothing, cars, motorcycles, rocks, insects

Find Them and Hidden Clothing ———————— DUPLICATORS 13 & 14

Objectives
scanning

Using the Page
1. Distribute the worksheet and do several examples together on the board.
2. Make up a worksheet using the names of some of the children in your class.
3. To make a more difficult worksheet, omit the answers at the top of the page.
4. To make an easier worksheet, put the answer at the end of each sentence, or have the words hidden within a longer word.

Creating Their Own
Create some together with the children so that they get the idea. Pick a topic such as names, clothing, sports, animals, or whatever interests your students. Start with the word, then figure out several logical divisions and include them in words. For example, the name "Tom" might be divided into To / m. The "m" can begin a word, such as *my*. "Go in**to m**y house and get the ball" would be a typical sentence that incorporates the name "Tom."

After you've done several together as a class, have your students make up some of their own sentences.

Additional Examples
1. Thi**s cot t**ilts when I roll over.
2. He spun the stra**w, and a**s he did, it turned to gold.
3. The he**ro y**earns for glory.
4. Bloody scenes make **one ill**.
5. Don't ta**ke it h**ard.
6. Make your be**d and** clean up your room.
7. When you go **to m**eet the queen, remember to bow.

Word Puzzle ————————————————————— DUPLICATOR 15

Objectives
scanning
finding logical shapes for words

Using the Page

1. Put some examples on the chalkboard and do them together with the class.

2. Make up some sentences using the names of children in your class.

3. For an easier worksheet, make shorter sentences.

Creating Their Own

Have the children write a sentence first. Rewrite the sentence dividing the words in irregular places. Make up a worksheet of the sentences the children have rewritten, or do them together on the chalkboard.

Additional Examples

1. Le tsh avel un chs aidt hesp i dert othe ef ly.
2. A llt hat glit tersi snot gol d.
3. Thes unsan kslo wlyi ntot hew est.

Kriss Kross ———————————————————————— DUPLICATOR 16

Objectives

scanning
spelling
categorizing
research

Using the Page

1. Make up a Kriss Kross using the names of the children in your class. You may want to make up a separate one for boys and girls. To make it more difficult, omit the names at the bottom of the page.

2. To make this worksheet easier, make the Kriss Kross smaller or fill in more of the answers.

3. These are easy to correct, because answers are right if they fit into the puzzle.

Creating Their Own

The children should select topics they're interested in. They can then make a list of words related to that topic. Their lists can come from resource materials, such as encyclopedias or books on the topic, or other relevant sources.

Once they have their list of words, the students should take a piece of graph paper and *in pen* create the Kriss Kross by writing in the answers, with words overlapping.

Then, have them outline the puzzle with a ruler and *pencil*. They should sign their names to the puzzles in pencil, too.

When you duplicate the puzzle, only the outline and signature in pencil will show. The student's original then becomes the answer key.

Additional Topics

birds, ice cream flavors, last names, trees, states, cities, countries, cereals, songs

Classifying

Crosses is a game of classifying and categorizing. Children are invited to generate words in various categories which begin with particular letters. This activity is for two persons, or teams of two.

Categories is a more sophisticated form of Crosses. The students decide the categories and letters in this game.

Word Lists is a list of words which the children must arrange in categories. Then they assign a title to each list.

Cookbook has a list of good-to-eat items which the students must assign to the correct cookbook heading.

Want Ads is a page with an actual want ad index on it. The children must decide under which main topic each item on a list of topics would appear.

Telephone Book involves finding various topics in the yellow pages.

The last three topics involve practical applications of categorizing. When children can see a need for learning something, it makes the learning more efficient and permanent.

Crosses and Categories ———————————————— DUPLICATORS 17 & 18

Objectives
> classifying

Using the Page
1. Play a game of crosses or categories on the board with the class.
2. Play a game with the class divided into two parts. One member from each team goes to the board and competes against the others for team points.
3. Have the children play individual games.

Creating Their Own
> Children draw their own grids, think of their own topics and letters, and compete against one another.

Additional Topics
> famous men, athletes, cities, parts of the body, TV programs, TV stars, fabrics

Word Lists

Objectives
> categorizing
> scanning

Using the Page
1. Put another list on the board and have the children arrange them into classifications together. Assign a title to each list.
2. To make the worksheet easier, put the topic headings on the page.
3. To make it more difficult, have the topics more closely related. Or, if your words lend themselves to this, after they have arranged the words into four lists, see if they can rearrange them into three lists, then into two.
4. To personalize them, use the names of children. Make your categories tall and short, blonde and brunette, etc.

Creating Their Own
Have the children make up three or four lists of words. Then they scramble the words, make one general list, and give these to others to classify. Make copies and distribute or have the students put them on the board for the other children to classify.

Additional Examples
> Insects—ant, bee, butterfly, aphid, cricket
> Mammals—man, monkey, horse, whale, cow
> Birds—eagle, bluejay, sparrow, dove, seagull
> Fish—perch, sailfish, tuna, cod, trout

Cookbook

Objectives
> classifying
> inferential thinking

Using the Page
1. Discuss different things the children like to eat and decide together under which title each belongs.
2. Have an actual recipe box with dividers in the room, and have the children bring favorite recipes and put them in the correct section.

Creating Their Own
Have the children list some of their favorite foods and give them to a friend to put into the correct section.

Additional Examples
> ice cream, candy bar, hamburger, carrots, mince pie, sausage

Want Ads ——————————————————————— DUPLICATOR 21

Objectives
>classification
>alphabetization

Using the Page
1. Discuss the various headings of the want ad index and what's included in each heading.
2. To make the worksheet easier, have the topics the same as those that appear in the index.
3. To make it more difficult, list objects more remotely related to main topics.
4. Put the main topics on the board. Read a want ad orally and have the children decide under which heading it goes.

Creating Their Own
>Have the children bring the want ad sections of their newspapers from home. Have them cut out the topics and paste them to a piece of a paper. They can locate different want ads, cut them out, and give them to a friend to place under the proper heading.

Additional Examples
>a transistor radio, a goldfish, piano lessons, a candy shop for sale, a mink coat

Telephone Book ——————————————————— DUPLICATOR 22

Objectives
>classifying
>alphabetical order

Using the Page
1. This page can be done without the telephone book, but, if you can, have the children bring old telephone books.
2. Discuss the reasons for having the yellow pages in the telephone book.
3. Elicit from the children comments on things they'd like to buy, and have them find them in the yellow pages.

Creating Their Own
>The children can think of things they'd like to buy, make a list, and have a friend decide where to get them. They can go through the yellow pages, list three or four things, and give the list to a friend to find.

>You can make a duplicator master of their lists or put them on the board for the rest of the class to locate.

Additional Examples
>baseball mitt, lawn mower, nurseries, candy stores

Comprehension and context clues

Nonsense Words in Sentences is an exercise in determining word meaning by using context clues. Children are asked to specify a reasonable meaning of the nonsense word.

Nonsense Words in a Story is much like the exercise above, except the nonsense words are used in a story, and child is asked to select appropriate meanings from a choice of four words.

Add-a-Letter is a group of sentences, each of which has two blanks. The child must determine the answer for one of the blanks by using context clues, then gets the other answer by adding or subtracting one letter.

Reading Choices is a comprehension activity in which the child is asked to answer who, what, when, or why questions from a set of multiple-choice answers. The structural clues in the question have to be used to find the answer.

Answers to Write Questions For is a reversal of the normal procedure. Children are usually asked to write answers to questions. This worksheet is an about-face that gives the answers, and lets the children supply the questions.

Nonsense Words in Sentences ———————————————— DUPLICATOR 23

Objectives
> using context clues
> using structural clues

Using the Page
> 1. Make up some samples of sentences using nonsense words, put them on the board, and do them together with the class.
> 2. Go over the worksheet together after the children have completed it.
> 3. Share the ones they have created orally.

Creating Their Own
> Have the children write three or four sentences, then replace one word in each sentence with a nonsense word. Make worksheets of the ones the children create.

Additional Examples

You should albop your dog every day.
Your mother will get zag if you blafp.
The papi grew out of the zazz.

Nonsense Words in a Story ———————————————— DUPLICATOR 24

Objectives

context clues

Using the Page

1. Use this page after the page on nonsense words in sentences.

2. Go over the page orally together after the children complete the worksheet. See if any other words make sense in the story.

3. Make up other worksheets by using original stories written by the children. Replace several of the words with nonsense words.

Creating Their Own

Have the children write short stories and replace several of the words with nonsense words. Have the children find short stories and rewrite them, replacing some of the words with nonsense words. Then make up worksheets of the ones the children have done, or share them orally.

Add-a-Letter ———————————————————— DUPLICATOR 25

Objectives

using context clues
spelling
logical letter combinations in words

Using the Page

1. Do some samples orally together.

2. To make the exercise easier, put synonyms under one or more of the blanks, or fill in one of the blanks for them. You can also scramble intermediate words and put them at the bottom of the page.

3. Make up a worksheet using names of some of the children in your class. Some examples might be: Tom—atom; Tim—time; Noel—novel; Sam—slam.

4. Correct the page orally together.

Creating Their Own

The children can make up lists of words. Start with a simple word such as *pan.* Then add a letter to make another word, such as *pain, pane* or *span.* Finally, they can use the two words in a sentence. It is important that their sentences give some clue to the answer that goes in one blank.

Share these sentences with the class, either orally or make up a worksheet.

Additional Examples

I *ran* inside the house because it began to *rain* and I didn't want to get wet.

My *plan* was to *plant* a new tree in the front yard.

The fish *bit* the *bait* and Henry reeled him into the boat.

Reading Choices ———————————————————— DUPLICATOR 26

Objectives
using structural clues to answer questions

Using the Page
1. Do some who, what, where, when, or why questions with the class orally. Have them give various possible answers to your questions.
2. Discuss the answers orally with the class after they have completed the worksheet.

Creating Their Own
Have the children write questions that begin with interrogative words. Then have them write three possible answers, only one of which directly answers the question.
Share these orally with the class or put students' work on a worksheet.

Additional Examples
1. Where is Jim?
   a. at 2 o'clock   b. by car   c. under the apple tree
2. How many were there?
   a. in the tree   b. four   c. a hot dog
3. Who jumped the farthest?
   a. the short fat boy   b. gray clouds   c. last year

Answers to Write Questions for ———————————— DUPLICATOR 27

Objectives
strengthening comprehension

Using the Page
1. Do some orally with the children first.
2. Go over the worksheet together after the children have completed it.
3. Share orally those they have created.

Creating Their Own
The children first write questions and answers to them. Then they give the answer to a friend and see if he can write a question to accompany the answer.

Additional Examples
outside in the rain
as much as I could
the best of them all
because the witch lost her broom

Prefix and suffix

GoFer is a list of polysyllabic words. The students are asked to "go fer" the root word and circle it. The practice is important in looking up words in the dictionary and for good spelling.

Pre- and Suf- fixes are practice sheets on prefixes, suffixes, and their meanings.

Cutoffs are words with parts cut off. The parts that are cut off look like prefixes but they aren't really. The confusion gives rise to some interesting "root words?"

Noords are words that don't exist, but have some form of legitimacy due to their conventional form and/or prefixes and suffixes. Guessing what the words mean provides some informative speculation on the part of the students.

GoFer —————————————————————————— DUPLICATOR 28

Objectives
> finding root words
> using the dictionary

Using the Page
1. List some long words and find the roots orally with the class.
2. Play a game. Give the children a common root word and have them make new words by adding prefixes and suffixes. The person with the most words wins. Words to use might be *like, run, pack, love, content, happy.*
3. To make the worksheet easier, add only a prefix or suffix, or put the answers at the bottom of the page.

Creating Their Own
> Have the children find several long words in the dictionary and circle the root words. Make a worksheet of their words or share them orally.

Additional Examples
> undistinguishable, unacceptable, exceptionally

Objectives

understanding prefixes
using the dictionary

Using the Page

1. Discuss prefixes and what they are.
2. Correct the worksheet orally with the class.
3. Play a game by dividing the class into two teams and giving the teams a common prefix. Have them list as many words as they can using the prefix. The team with the most words wins a point. Possible prefixes are pre-, im-, in-, re-, dis-, un-.

Creating Their Own

Have the children select a prefix from the dictionary. Then have them make a page, listing the prefixes followed by a blank and the definition. Encourage them to use common words both as definitions and as unknowns. Prepare a worksheet of their words or share them orally with the rest of the class.

Additional Examples

ex ___*act*___ is precise

ex ___*amine*___ is to look closely

ex ___*haust*___ is to tire

ex ___*port*___ is to send out

ex ___*pert*___ is a professional

ex ___*ist*___ is to be

ex *hibitionist* is a show-off

Objectives

understanding prefixes and suffixes
word meaning

Using the Page

1. Discuss meaning of prefixes and suffixes. Do some examples together.
2. Play a game with three sets of flash cards. Make up one set with prefixes, one set with root words, and one set with suffixes. Give a child one of the root word cards, and see how quickly he can add an appropriate prefix and suffix to it.
3. Go over the worksheet orally with the children after they have done it.

Creating Their Own

Have the children find words with suffixes and write the meanings. Make a worksheet of the children's examples or share them orally with the class.

Additional Examples

<u>*cheer*</u>   ful is happy

<u>*help*</u>   ful is assisting

<u>*beauti*</u>   ful is lovely

<u>*care*</u>   ful is cautious

<u>*doubt*</u>   ful is skeptical

Cutoffs —————————————————— DUPLICATOR 31

Objectives

creating meanings
using the dictionary

Using the Page

1. These are just nonsense words, but the children can make reasonable guesses at their meanings. A reasonable guess takes into account the meaning of the prefix or suffix as well as the "feel" of the root word. Do some examples orally together to demonstrate the process.

2. Go over the worksheet orally together when the class has completed it.

3. Encourage the children to use these words in sentences after they have decided what they mean.

Creating Their Own

The children can look up prefixes in the dictionary to use in their own nonsense words. Some examples they might start with are trans-, tele-, dis-, pre-, re-, fore-, and un-. Share their work with the class.

Additional Examples

pare (as in prepare)   tent (as in content)
ite (as in unite)   lieve (as in believe)
gion (as in region)

Noords —————————————————— DUPLICATOR 32

Objectives

using prefixes and suffixes

Using the Page

1. Encourage the children to make up words. Decide what they mean. Use them in sentences. Write their definitions on the board. Use the nonsense words in your daily conversation. For example, make up a new word for pencil and encourage the children to use the new word in its place.

2. Go over the worksheet orally after the children have completed it.

Creating Their Own

The children should make up their own nonsense words. Share these as above or in a worksheet.

Additional Examples

unknuckle, replock, skyful, fenceable, discouch, retrunk

Structural analysis

Word Compounds are pictures that name the two parts of a compound word. This is an introductory exercise for thinking about compounds.

Togetherness presents two words that are synonyms for the parts of a compound word. The synonyms do not give a definition of the parts of the compound; they merely evoke the words that form the compound word.

Fill in the Blanks is an exercise that asks the students to expand from a common combination of letters to form words incorporating that combination.

More Add-a-Letter stretches the students' spelling ability by giving words to which another letter has to be added to form a different word. Experiments with different placements of the letter to be added give the student lots of opportunity to spell words to see if they make sense.

Add-a-Letter Sentences expands on the previous exercise by asking students to add one letter to several words in a sentence, making new words and a sensible sentence.

Step Words carries the skill one step further by asking the student to change a given beginning word one letter at a time until it forms a totally different word. Each of the intermediate words must be a legitimate English word.

Word Compounds ——————————————————————— DUPLICATOR 33

Objectives

      synonyms
      understanding compound words

Using the Page

1. Discuss compound words as a combination of two words, not necessarily meaning the same thing as the original two words. *Boy* and *play* both mean something, but put them together as *playboy* and they come to mean something entirely different. A *ball* is something to play with and a *screw* is a threaded metal fastener, but a *screwball* is an entirely different matter. See if the class can come up with some of these combinations.

2. Show how compound words are different from words with prefixes and suffixes. *Playmate* is a compound word, but *playful* is a root word with a suffix. *Payroll* is a compound word, but *repay* is a prefix plus a root word. Try to find other examples with the class.

3. After doing the page, the class should be able to discuss their answers and possible differences among them.

Creating Their Own

Before the students begin creating their own, it would be a good idea to discuss what sorts of compound words might make good pictures. Point out that *shoelace* or *shoehorn* would be easy to draw, but that *highlight* or *sidewinder* might be hard to show with pictures. They should also think about whether one or two pictures are appropriate to show the compound word. Words such as *sailboat* and *airport* are better drawn with one drawing then with two. Ask whether these words are better shown with one or two drawings, or are very hard to draw a picture for at all: lonesome, airplane, pineapple, peanut, overload, candlestick, doorknob, handsome, motorcycle, plywood, batman.

You might also discuss the difficulties of drawing such complex things as pictures for *daydream* or *warfare*.

Additional Examples

Additional examples are included in the previous section.

Togetherness ————————————————————

Objectives

compound words
finding synonyms
using the thesaurus and dictionary

Using the Page

1. Since the words on the page are not definitions of parts of the compound words, and in many cases are not even similes, you might explain the difference between word association and definition. If I say "boot" and you say "cowboy," your word *cowboy* is an association for boot, but it is certainly not a definition of boot. Likewise with the first problem on the page–"boot" might suggest "shoe," and "tie" could recall "lace," giving "shoelace" as the answer for the two words, *boot* and *tie*.

2. After the students do the page, go over it orally and see if they came up with different compound words for the same pair of words.

3. Make up a duplicator master of the students' examples, or do them orally with the class.

Creating Their Own

Students should think of the compound word first, then try to think of two related words that go with the compound word. Working the other way, from the two words to the compound, is much more difficult.

Additional Examples

pony	bird	*horsefly*	tummy	snap	*bellybutton*
war	boat	*battleship*	milk	blow	*creampuff*
halt	clock	*stopwatch*	heaven	bulb	*skylight*
sky	smooth	*airplane*	shoe	lumber	*sandalwood*
angry	amble	*crosswalk*			

Fill in the Blanks ————————————————————————

Objectives

using definitions

seeing how a letter pair can make a different sound in different words

Using the Page

1. Write a pair of letters on the board, a vowel followed by a consonant. "On" or "ut" might be good combinations. Then see how many different words the class can think of that have this letter combination in it. **On**e, **t**on, **s**on, **pon**y, **on**ly, **gon**e, **mon**ey all incorporate "on," and "ut" is in b**ut**, h**ut**, m**ut**, b**ut**ton, b**ut**ter, and lots of others. Show them how to make the blanks indicating the letters needed to complete the word.

2. Play a game in which the two sides are given the same vowel-consonant combination, and challenge each other to guess the word they are thinking of, given the blanks and an informal definition.

3. Correct the worksheet orally and see if anyone can find a different word that fits the definition.

Creating Their Own

Have the students pick a vowel-consonant combination, then write a list of words that have that combination in them. Then have them write an informal definition of each word. Finally, they should recopy the words using blanks for all letters but the given combination, and writing the informal definition beside each word.

Additional Examples

h at   what you cover your head with

b at   what you strike out with

c at   what you give milk in a dish

s at   what you did when you were too tired to stand

f l at   not rough

f or *e s t*   where little Red Riding Hood got lost

p or *t*   where boats are unloaded

s c or *e*   what you get for a touchdown

f l o or   what keeps you out of the basement

More Add-a-Letter ————————————————————————

Objectives

finding logical forms of words

adding sounds to letter groups

using the dictionary

Using the Page

1. Do the first group of words orally with the class. Show them that the letter *f* can be added to *lie* in a number of places, but that *flie* is not a correct spelling for *fly,* and that *lief* is not the correct spelling for *life.* If they're unsure, they should look up a combination in the dictionary or in their speller to make sure. The only place that *f* can be added to *lie* to correctly spell a word is between the *i* and the *e* for *life.* Try the other words in the list, and see what combinations they can come up with that sound like words, but that aren't correctly spelled. Have them write the correctly spelled words to the right of the letter combinations.

2. When the students have made up a set of their own, either put them on the board for others to try out, or make a duplicator master. Since the letter combinations are difficult to visualize, the exercise should not be done orally.

Creating Their Own

Have the students make a long list of words that all contain the same common letter. Then have them rewrite each word without that common letter. They can use a dictionary if they need to check whether the remaining letters spell a word. Have them circle the correctly spelled letter combinations. Then have them rewrite the circled words in a list, with the common missing letter at the top of the list.

Additional Examples

d		s	
one	*done*	lad	*s*
an	*and*	path	*s*
ear	*dear*	lane	*s*
see	*seed*	at	*sat*
rip	*drip*	plaid	*s*

Add-a-Letter Sentences ——————————————— DUPLICATOR 37

Objectives

logical shapes of words
trying different combinations of letters
using context clues

Using the Page

1. Write a sentence on the blackboard, such as "The seven fast sloops went west slowly." Then erase the letter *s* every time it appears. Now read the sentence with the class, and show that it makes no sense, even though all the words in it are really words. Then show how adding the letter *s* to one of the words changes that word, and keep adding *s* to the other words until the sentence makes sense.

2. Do the same with the first sentence on the worksheet, so that everyone understands how to do it.

3. To make the worksheet easier, write the letter to be added under each word it should be added to.

4. To make the worksheet harder, omit the missing letter *before* the sentence, so that they have to figure out which letter is missing, as well as where it goes.

Creating Their Own

Have the students follow the same procedure that you did in introducing the page. They should write out a sentence with a number of words containing a common letter, then erase that letter each time it appears. Finally, they should recopy the sentence so the spacing doesn't give a clue about where the missing letters appear.

Additional Examples

B   Don't eat ^b^lue ^b^erries from the ^b^ushes.

L   A^ll^ the ^l^itt^l^e nuts fe^ll^ through a ^l^hoe in the bow^l^.

K   Stac^k^ the blac^k^berries bac^k^ on the rac^k^.

M   ^m^End ^m^ore of ^m^oys ^mm^at^m^ches to for ^m^an^m^y ^m^arionettes.

g   ^g^One are the ^g^ray days of dra^gg^ing ba^g^s bu^g^ling with ^g^rain from the ^g^round to the loft.

Step Words ────────────────────────────

Objectives

spelling
trying different letter combinations

Using the Page

1. Write a simple word on the board, such as *bag*. Ask the children if they can think of another word that is different from *bag* by only one letter. When someone comes up with a word, such as *bar*, write it on the board—and see if they can think of another word that is different from *bar* by only one letter. Keep this word chain going as long as you can.

2. Write *boy* on the board, and leave a good bit of space before you write *man* underneath it. Explain that you would like to make a word chain like the one you did earlier, only this time you'd like the words to go from *boy* to *man*. What are some words that might come in between? They might suggest, *toy*, which may evoke *tan* from the last word. Finally the word *ton* comes between *toy* and *tan*, as the link that allows you to change only one letter at a time. The series, then, is *boy toy ton tan man*. Show them that each word differs from the word before it by only one letter.

3. Correct the worksheet *visually* by writing suggested answers on the board. Show that there can be more than one correct solution, and that some are longer than others.

4. Make up a duplicator master of the ones the students made, and give copies to the class; or have the students put the ones they made up on the board for others to solve.

Creating Their Own

Have the students pick two related words that have the same number of letters. Then let them try to transform one of the words into the other. If they get stumped, they can try to begin at the other word and go backwards. Have them write their solutions and turn them in as well as the beginning and end words.

Additional Examples

PAT	HOT	EYE	COWS
pot	*pot*	*dye*	*bows*
dot	*pat*	*doe*	*boas*
_____	_____	*dot*	*boat*
		sot	*moat*
DOG	PAN	*sat*	_____
		set	MEAT
		_____	
		SEE	

T_T

Scrambled words

By trying many combinations of letters to form words, the students test many more words than they would in a conventional spelling lesson.

Rambledscword gives the students scrambled combinations of letters that they must make into correctly spelled words. Practice with the many possible orders of the letters gives the students a feel for the likely "correct" shapes of words, as well as dictionary practice verifying their guesses.

Scrambleword Sentences give the student a chance to turn the same scrambled letters into two words that fit into the context of a sentence.

Wordswordsinwords gives the student a chance to exercise his skill in the opposite way, picking letters out of a word, then scrambling them and reforming a smaller word.

Palindromes give the student an imaginative exercise, trying to figure out common words that are the same spelled backwards or forwards.

Reverse takes the reversal skill one step further, asking the students to find words that are meaningful both backwards and forwards, and that fit into a sentence. These words are different from palindromes in that they are not the same backwards as forwards.

Rambledscword ———————————————————————— DUPLICATOR 39

Objectives

spelling
trying various combinations of letters

Using the Page

1. Give out the worksheet, and see if the students can make up more than one word from the scrambled letters.
2. Ask the students to make up some of their own, and put them on a worksheet—or have them put them on the board.

Creating Their Own

Ask the students for a simple word. Write it on the board. Then scramble the letters. Show them how some scramblings are more difficult than others.

They can also play a game of team competition, in which one team gives a scrambled word to the others, and the team that unscrambles it first gets a point.

Additional Examples

viseg *(gives)*   drore *(order)*   tobos *(boots)*   certap *(carpet)*   lokcc *(clock)*

petelohen *(telephone)*   rugas *(sugar)*   coratucall *(calculator)*   gristikn *(striking)*

Scrambleword sentences ———————————————— DUPLICATOR 40

Objectives
context clues
spelling

Using the Page
1. Do an example or two with the class. If it seems difficult, give them these clues for the last five sentences. tac—4. enma—5. art—6. onmel—7. acer—8. speta—9.
2. Ask the students to make up their own sentences and turn them in.

Creating Their Own
Have the students think up two words that comprise the same letters. Write the two words on the blackboard and make up a sentence using the words. Then erase the words. If the class has difficulty with the exercise, scramble the words and put them at the beginning of the sentence.

Additional Examples
tews—When he cooks_____, the chef always_____ the pan with cooking oil.

selpo—While she was racing down the_____, the skier used her_____ to keep her balance.

askcl—One man alone_____the strength to take up the_____ in a telephone line.

Wordswordsinwords ————————————————— DUPLICATOR 41

Objectives
spelling
using definitions

Using the Page
1. Go over the answers to the first few examples to make sure the students understand where the letters in the answers come from.
2. Explain that the letters in the given word may only be used one time. They couldn't get *tattoo* out of *potatoes,* for example, because *potatoes* doesn't have three *t*s.
3. Let them use a dictionary if they like. They can start by looking up a letter in the word, then checking to see if all the other letters in the dictionary word are in the given word.

Creating Their Own
Put a big word on the blackboard, and have students try to make words out of the letters in it. They might just call out definitions, and see if other students can figure out the word. For younger children, the first letter can be given as well as the definition. For older children, the number of letters in the word can be omitted.

Palindromes ———————————————————————— DUPLICATOR 42

Objectives
spelling
left–right orientation
vocabulary

Using the Page
1. Spell the examples on the blackboard. Read them to the students backwards, and have them write them, or rewrite them on the board. Demonstrate that they're the same backwards as forwards.
2. Palindromes are hard to think up, so they might try to look some up in a small dictionary, or do them together.

Additional Examples
a crazy person—kook
a silencer—gag
what a cork does when you open a bottle—pop

Reverse ———————————————————————————— DUPLICATOR 43

Objectives
context clues
spelling

Using the Page
1. Have the students do the worksheet so they understand the concept of reversing the letters in one word to make the other.
2. Ask them to make up a few sentences of their own, leaving a blank where the two reversed words go in the sentence.

Creating Their Own
When the students make up their own sentences, figuring out words that are also words backwards will be the most difficult part. Once they have a pair in mind, they should think of a sentence that incorporates both words. Younger students, or ones having more difficulty with the concept, can write definitions under each blank.

Additional Examples

I wonder where I _laid_ my pencil when I went to _dial_ the telephone number?

The people in canoes were _mad_ when they ran into a _dam_ across the river.

When he saw it wasn't a comet, the man looking through a telescope said, "Oh, _rats_,

it's just a _star_ .

Alphabetization

Scrambled Sentences are zany sentences that only make sense when they are unscrambled in alphabetical order.

Classified Ads are cut-up advertisements which show the students the practical application of alphabetization skills. Want-ads from the local newspaper can be used to extend this activity.

Telephone Book gives students the realistic task of looking up people in the telephone book. They can then be asked to find classmates' phone numbers and to think up other important things to find the telephone number for.

Scrambled Sentences ───────────────────────────── DUPLICATOR 44

Objectives
> alphabetization
> synonyms

Using the Page
> 1. Work the first example on the board, putting the words in an alphabetized list. Then write the list in sentence form, so the students see that it indeed makes a sentence.
> 2. Have the students make up their own sentences, then check to see whether they are alphabetized.

Creating Their Own
> When the students make up sentences, they should just try for a fairly long sentence, made up of prepositions and structural words that are in general order, not worrying about the nouns or verbs especially. Then they should think of synonyms or zany words that are in the proper alphabetical order to substitute for the ones that are not ordered correctly.
>
> After they've got an alphabetized list, the students can scramble the words and give the list to somebody else.
>
> For more difficult problems, they can have some of the words with matching first, second, and third letters. Sentences that have words all of which begin with different letters are the easiest to work.

Additional Examples

far, be, home, always, from, careful, going

bothers, riverbanks, but, balmy, can't, Betty, on, catch, bottles, crayfish

Classified Ads ───────────────────────────────── DUPLICATOR 45

Objectives
alphabetization

Using the Page
1. Show the students how to tear the sections apart with a ruler (or make sure there are enough pairs of scissors for them to use). Have them cut the ads apart into groups, then reassemble them in alphabetical order. When they are sure the ads are in order, they can tape them in a long column.

2. You can compare the difficulty of finding an item when they are alphabetized versus unalphabetized by playing a game. Have one group use their ads in an ordered column. Have another group use their ads cut apart and spread randomly across their desks. Then call out a car and a year—and the first team to call out the price gets the point. The children will see that the team that has them alphabetized has a tremendous advantage.

Creating Their Own
The students can bring in all sorts of alphabetized sections of the paper—the obituaries, births, the stock market quotations—and cut them apart for others to alphabetize.

Telephone Book ───────────────────────────────── DUPLICATOR 46

Objectives
alphabetization
locating names in reference materials

Using the Page
1. If you don't want the students to cut up the page, have them write the phone number of the first person listed with that last name. If there is no person with the last name, then have them write *none* after the name.

2. The same page can be used again, having the students look up the last name listed under that spelling.

3. If the students cut up their worksheets into strips with a name on each strip, they will find that when the strips are in the phone book in the proper place, all the strips are alphabetized.

Creating Their Own
Students can cut up ten or fifteen strips, and write the first and last name of a person on the strip. They can make an answer key with the person's name and phone number on it. Then they can give the strips to somebody to look up in the phone book.

Nyms

Homonames introduces homonyms as names that are used as proper, given names as well as a common noun. The students can go on to finding a common meaning for their own names.

Name Sounds the Same leaves homonyms out of sentences, but gives the students a clue under each word that is left out.

Antonyms allows the student the choice of words in a sentence that he or she wants to contradict. Emphasis in this exercise is on the making of meaningful, coherent sentences by changing only one word.

Homonames ——————————————————— DUPLICATOR 47

Objectives
synonyms
using definitions
homonyms

Using the Page
You can introduce the page by picking out the names of some of your students that have simple meanings. If you have a Bob in your class, for example, you might ask the students if the word *bob* means anything other than a boy's name. Writing it on the board in lower case letters gives the students the idea that the word can appear in a different context. If they come up with the definition (to bounce up and down on water), you might ask them to see if somebody else's name means something. Bill, Mary, Pete, and Pat are all names that sound like common words. In every class so far we've found John insuppressible, and the chances for its coming up are good.

Creating Their Own
Ask the students to pick out a name—theirs, or that of someone they know. If they begin with the name, then try to think of a word that sounds the same, they are much more likely to be successful than if they try to think of a name that means a specific word. If the students use last names of others in the class, they shouldn't be too difficult. Using any last name can become quite difficult.

Additional Examples

money—Penny	hirsute—Harry
duck's nose—Bill	valley—Dale
go up and down on water—Bob	tote—Kerry
G.I. doll—Joe	rabbit home—Warren
sunlight—Ray	fade—Wayne
something good to eat—Candy	a haystack—Rick
hit softly—Pat	covered with tiny dirt particles—Sandy
a little word, same as "a"—Ann	surface-to-air missile—Sam

The Name Sounds the Same ———————————— DUPLICATOR 48

Objectives

using context clues
finding homonyms
using synonyms

Using the Page

If the students need some review, remind them that some words are spelled differently but sound the same (words like *their* and *there* or *road* and *rode*). If the page seems too easy, ask them to try the sentences without looking at the definitions. If the page is difficult, show the students how pinpointing one word they're sure of allows them to search for the homonym that fits in the other blank. In sentence one, they might think that *fur* means *hair*, and use that one word they're more sure of to get the more obscure homonym, *hare*.

Creating Their Own

The process indicated on the page is fairly simple. When they've thought of a pair of homonyms, the students can make up a sentence using the pair. When they write their definitions, ask them to be sure that the definitions fit in the blank. It's a good study in context clues.

Additional Examples

1. They put a _*steel*_ bar across the door so nobody could get in and _*steal*_ his new

metal   take
    radio.

2. If your _*brake*_ doesn't work, you might _*break*_ your car.

         stopper   crash

3. A _*bear*_ got in our tent and cleaned the cooler _*bare*_ .

  furry animal   empty

4. They found a _*sail*_ for their boat on _*sale*_ at the store.

          canvas   discount

5. Have you _*seen*_ where they shot this _*scene*_ from the movie?

          viewed   picture

6. The bloodhound was _*sent*_ to search for the _*scent*_ of the lost, rare _*cent*_ .

                dispatched   odor   coin

7. He poured a _*vial*_ of _*vile*_ smelling liquid on his base _*viol*_ to bring the

         bottle   foul   string instrument
    lustrous sound out of the wood.

Objectives

> antonyms
> context clues
> synonyms

Using the Page

1. Show the students that in the first sentence there are several words that could be replaced with their opposites. "The man went OFF a diet because he was so thin," or "The man went on a diet because he was so FAT," or "The man went on a diet ALTHOUGH he was so thin."

2. Have the students try to see different places in the sentences that they could substitute opposites to make the sentence more accurate.

Creating Their Own

Ask the class to come up with a sentence. Write it on the board. Then cross out one word and in its place write its opposite. Now look at the sentence, and see which of several corrections could be made to make the sentence correct.

Additional Examples

The clock chimes three times at four o'clock since it always told the right time.

When you get up in the morning, you are likely to be tired.

Poetic diction

Alliteration is a prosaic approach to a poetic skill. The exercise sensitizes students to alliteration, which is used in advertisements, in slogans, and in nonsense stories.

Kennings are an old poetic device that make strange, imaginative expressions stand for prosaic objects. The exercise reinforces noun and verb distinctions, as well as stretching the creative imagination of the students.

Draw-a-Word allows the students to draw the meaning of a word by stretching the graphics of the letters. The words on the page are just a starting point for the students' own forays into their vocabularies.

Draw-a-Poem asks the students to express the literal meaning of the poem in the way the words are written on the page. This is a good follow-up activity for haiku or free verse, and a good introduction to e.e. cummings or other graphic poets.

Alliteration ——————————————————————— DUPLICATOR 50

Objectives
> using alliteration
> finding synonyms
> using the dictionary and thesaurus

Using the Page
> This is the sort of page that goes over well on a rainy day when the students are ready to do something a little giddy.

> Begin by noticing that sometimes words all start with the same letter, and that this is called alliteration. Write a simple sentence on the board, such as "Mother went to the store to buy some peanut butter." Pick a single word in the sentence that begins with the letter you want to alliterate with and then begin finding synonyms for other words that begin with the same letter. If *p* from *peanut* was chosen, the children might replace *mother* with *parent, buy* might become *purchase,* and *went* could be replaced with *paced.* A dictionary or thesaurus is a good source of ideas for alliterative words. Finally, a sentence such as "a popular parent perused packed panoramas to purchase powdered peanut protein," might emerge in the place of the more mundane, "mother went to the store to buy some peanut butter." A little frivolous, perhaps, but certainly more imaginative.

Creating Their Own

Students making up their own alliterative sentences can use the method outlined above, or they can just begin with a letter and let their imaginations flow. One of a student's own initials is often a good starting point. Make sure that they understand that prepositions and articles don't have to alliterate—though they may want to eliminate as many of them that don't as possible. See who can come up with the longest sentence.

Additional Examples

Some super strong soap softly dissolved the skin.

Ken quickly capped key Coke cans.

Ben bent and bound banded bunches of bananas.

Instantly, Imogene imaginatively imitated an imposter insinuating herself into an initiation.

Prejudicial pretrial publicity plummeted prospects for perjury prosecution.

Sarah, Sandy, and Susie sassed sassafras sippers as they sashayed smoothly by.

Kennings ———————————————————— DUPLICATOR 51

Objectives

inference
using subject-verb relationships
imaginative language

Using the Page

Read this section of a poem to your class, and ask students to pick out kennings and other imaginative expressions:

> *Widsith, the Minstrel*
> *Widsith spoke, his word-hoard unlocked,*
> *Who most had traveled of men on earth . . .*
>
> *In his earliest travels*
> *With Ealhild he went, fair weaver of peace,*
> *From the East out of Angle to Eormanric's home,*
> *Who was prince of the Goths, fierce breaker of pledges.*
> *Many a tale he told of his travels . . . . ***

Discuss the verb-object relationship that makes up a kenning, and the way in which kennings are more descriptive, more dynamic than adjectives.

Creating Their Own

Ask your students to pick a common object, say a plate. Then ask what action is associated with the object. A plate is a "server" or perhaps a "holder." Then ask what thing, what object is associated with that object. A plate holds *food.* Putting the two together, a plate might be called a "food-holder." Then refine the kenning by asking what other things might be included in that kenning. Our example might fit a serving dish, a refrigerator, or can. See if there isn't some characteristic that will limit the kenning—"shallow" or "flattened" might be added to "food-holder".

The resulting equivalent often shows something about the writer's point of view that is much more provocative than the statement of the simple noun that the kenning stands for.

*From an anthology of Old English Poetry, translated by Charles W. Kennedy, 1960, Oxford University Press, p. 59.

Objectives

> inferential thinking
> visualization of a word

Using the Page

> This activity could be started off by thinking of various words, verbs or adjectives, and imagining what they mean. Take the word *square* as an example. The students could make the letters entirely out of squares, or write the word around the perimeter of a square. The word *loops* might be done so all the round letters have loops that interlock, like this:

LOOPS

> Once students get the idea, they can do all sorts of things with printing the word to show the effect of the word.

Creating Their Own

> There are a number of ways students can use a word to begin a graphic representation of itself. They can pick out one letter to present the word—

TIE   Knot   baseball

> Or they can make the letters do what the word says—

GROW

> They can draw the letters in a way that suggests the word—

Rope   TENSION   BREAK

> Or they can make the word look like the thing it represents:

bell   BOX   CIRCLE

> They can also draw additions that artistically suggest results of the word:

sad   BEC   SPLASH

Objectives

> inferential thinking
> visualizing a sentence

Using the Page

> Discuss the string of words that leads up to the kite and the sag that it mentions. The lesson might be used to reinforce haiku, or as a preliminary to it. The brevity of the poem is important, and the visualization is all-important. Records with lots of visual images, pictures of scenes, and haiku are all materials that can be used to conjure up creative settings.

Creating Their Own

Once students have visualized a setting, they can write a brief description of it. Ask them to omit all nonessentials, to strip the description to the bare outlines of the scene. Then try to imagine the physical outlines. Chances are that they will have to make several false starts before one of the "poems" evokes something they can depict graphically. Tenacity, patience, and encouragement will all come in handy.

Additional Examples

The rain comes down in little thin strings that sag in the wind.

The tree in the middle of the road has cars going around it on both sides.

The candle is big and fat and solid and it doesn't move; the flame wiggles.

Potpourri

These old-time favorite games are perfect for a rainy day, for a pick-me-up in the middle of a day that is dragging.

007 Strikes Again starts the students out cracking codes that progress from simple to not-so-simple-at-all. Once they get going, you'll never read the notes they pass again.

What Are They? They're droodles—simple, whimsical drawings that demand a different perspective for their offbeat interpretation. You don't have to be an artist to make them up—but you do have to see things from a different vantage point.

Letter-Word asks the students to interpret letters of the alphabet as syllables in words.

License Plates allows the students to see what happens when adults use Letter-Words in combinations with numbers to make expressive statements on their cars. The students can start a collection of the ones they see on the streets.

Hangman is an old favorite spelling game. Just in case you've forgotten the rules, or in case your students need a rulesheet in front of them, here it is.

007 Strikes Again ———————————————— DUPLICATOR 54

Objectives

        spelling
        scanning

Using the Page

1. Explain that each code sentence says something. They are to find out what the code is, and what the sentence says.

2. Make up a code in class, showing the students how the code has to be a system. Let them know that extremely difficult codes use different symbols for the same letter, but that the ones they'll be reading all have only one symbol for each letter.

3. For easier codes, put the symbols in the order they are to be read. Harder codes start from the middle and work out, or are every fourth letter of the original sentence, or other complicated patterns. Stress pattern.

Creating Their Own

Have the students make up a sentence. Then, if they can't think of a code of their own, have them use one of the codes on the page. As a check, make sure they translate the sentence from code back to English.

tsohg eht dnuora dewohs thgin eht ni skraps

up gjoe uif ijeefo usfbtvsf, xbnl pwfs up uif esjoljoh gpvoubjo cz uif pggjdf boe nppl voefs ju.

Tpueieeetiu lhop cshseqleripk pw eus cnrlplihqri.

Answers to the examples:

Sparks in the night showed around the ghost.

To find the hidden treasure, walk over to the drinking fountain by the office and look under it.

The porcupine prickles people with his queer quills.

What Are They?————————————————— DUPLICATOR 55

Objectives

seeing ambiguity

humor

visualizing a different point of view

Using the Page

1. Show how they can interpret a picture in several ways. Draw the picture at the right, and then show them that it could be part of several different bigger drawings.

2. Get them to begin to try a few of the pictures. See who can make up the most imaginative title.

Creating Their Own

Have them imagine an unusual situation, then draw just a detail of that situation. Taking different points of view—an ant's, a giant's, a bird's—is a good way of thinking up new droodles.

Additional Examples

A fat man's view of his feet.

Supercow

An ant carrying a peanut on his back, seen from above.

Letter-Word

Objectives
> spelling
> long vowel sounds

Using the Page
> 1. Ask the students to name some words that are also the names of letters. Show them both the spelling of the word and the letter that the word sounds like.
> 2. Have them do the worksheet, or do the exercises orally as a class.

Creating Their Own
> The students can use the letter-words at the top of the page to make up sentences with. Have them think of two or three that they want to work into a sentence, then write the sentence around the words they picked.

Additional Examples
> G EV climbed the IV.
>
> B4 U go, write an EZ SA.

License Plates

Objectives
> spelling
> verbal association
> inferential thinking

Using the Page
> 1. Read some of the license plates with the class. Ask them who might have a plate that says that on his or her car. Ask them if any of them have personalized plates. What personalized plates have they seen that are interesting?
> 2. Make up some in class, and see who they fit.

Creating Their Own
> Think of a short phrase or word that typifies a particular occupation or person. Then see if there is a way to get that phrase or word on a license plate, using numbers, letter-words, or parts of words.

Additional Examples
> METRE—math teacher
> GLU SHU—jockey
> DC 10—pilot
> DRV SAF—driver ed. teacher

Objectives

        spelling

Using the Page

1.   Play a game of hangman with the class. You might use *hangman* as your word to begin with. Show them that they have to start with the correct number of blanks—one for each letter in the word. Make sure that they understand that when a letter is guessed, it has to be written in the word as many times as it appears.

2.   After they've played a few games, get together for a strategy session. Do you want a long word? If so, do you want one with lots of vowels or a few vowels? What letters do people guess a lot? Why? If you see an *s* in a word, what things are likely to come after it? What letters are unlikely to come after *s*?

Additional Ideas

        Play the game in teams. Keep score. To make it easier, add body parts that have to be on before the man is hung—eyes, nose, mouth, boots, a hat, etc.

Rhymies

Find two rhyming words that mean the same thing.

_____*One ton*_____ 2000 pounds

_____*bug rug*_____ insect carpet

_____ metal lawn

_____ chubby kitten

_____ cat glove

_____ warm place

_____ metal smile

_____ mean boy

_____ silly rabbit

_____ tuna plate

_____ tall hairpiece

_____ bad pants

_____ tin pot

_____ steal angel food

_____ rose strength

_____ lad plaything

_____ empty rocker

_____ load bag

_____ tiny corridor

_____ fine fudge

_____ unkind lima

_____ rat home

_____ wet light

Make up a few of your own. Try them out on somebody.

_____   _____   _____   _____

_____   _____   _____   _____

_____   _____   _____   _____

Rhymies

Find two rhyming words that mean the same thing.

One ton —— 2000 pounds

bug rug —— insect carpet

brass grass —— metal lawn

fat cat —— chubby kitten

kitten mitten —— cat glove

hot spot —— warm place

tin grin —— metal smile

bad lad —— mean boy

funny bunny —— silly rabbit

fish dish —— tuna plate

big wig —— tall hairpiece

mean jeans —— bad pants

metal kettle —— tin pot

take cake —— steal angel food

flower power —— rose strength

boy toy —— lad plaything

bare chair —— empty rocker

pack sack —— load bag

small hall —— tiny corridor

dandy candy —— fine fudge

mean bean —— unkind lima

mouse house —— rat home

damp lamp —— wet light

Make up a few of your own. Try them out on somebody.

_____ _____   _____ _____

_____ _____   _____ _____

_____ _____   _____ _____

Rhyming Animals

Name _____

Fill in the blanks with an animal's name and a word that sounds the same.

1. The _____*Cat*_____ was too _____*fat*_____ from eating mice.

2. The _____ had a bad _____ of chewing carrots with his mouth open.

3. I know a _____ is _____ because I can see his antlers.

4. The _____ will _____ if you play with her cubs.

5. We _____ the _____ singing behind the fence.

6. The cat ate the _____ out of his _____ .

7. The _____ flew too _____ and hit the telephone wires.

8. The _____ _____ likes to _____ in the mud.

9. Mama _____ cleaned out her _____ so her babies would have a nice place to live.

Make one up yourself. Name an animal and a word that rhymes with it.

_____   _____

Use these two in a sentence. Write it below and give it to a friend to figure out.

_____

Rhyming Animals

Name _____

Fill in the blanks with an animal's name and a word that sounds the same.

1. The _____*cat*_____ was too _____*fat*_____ from eating mice.

2. The _____*rabbit*_____ had a bad _____*habit*_____ of chewing carrots with his mouth open.

3. I know a _____*deer*_____ is _____*near*_____ because I can see his antlers.

4. The _____*bear*_____ will _____*care*_____ if you play with her cubs.

5. We _____*heard*_____ the _____*bird*_____ singing behind the fence.

6. The cat ate the _____*fish*_____ out of his _____*dish*_____ .

7. The _____*crow*_____ flew too _____*low*_____ and hit the telephone wires.

8. The _____*big*_____ _____*pig*_____ likes to _____*dig*_____ in the mud.

9. Mama _____*mouse*_____ cleaned out her _____*house*_____ so her babies would have a nice place to live.

Make one up yourself. Name an animal and a word that rhymes with it.

_____   _____

Use these two in a sentence. Write it below and give it to a friend to figure out.

_____

"Oh, You Can't Get to Heaven" Name_____

You may have heard the old song, "Oh, You Can't Get to Heaven," but even if you haven't, you can still play the game that goes along with it.

Each verse begins, "You can't get to Heaven . . ." and you fill in a way you could go.

The second line gives some reason why you can't get to Heaven that way, and has to rhyme with the last word of the first line.

Here are a few examples:

Oh, you can't get to Heaven _*in a rocking chair*_

'cause _*the Lord don't want no lazy folks there,*_

Oh, you can't get to Heaven _*in a big balloon*_

'cause _*the gosh-darn thing will get stuck on the moon.*_

Try finishing the last line of these:

Oh, you can't get to Heaven _*on a city bus*_

'cause _____

Oh, you can't get to Heaven _*in a little rowboat*_

'cause _____

Oh, you can't get to Heaven _*in a motor car*_

'cause _____

See if you can make up one of your own.

Oh, you can't get to Heaven _____

'cause _____

"Oh, You Can't Get to Heaven" Name_____

You may have heard the old song, "Oh, You Can't Get to Heaven," but even if you haven't, you can still play the game that goes along with it.

Each verse begins, "You can't get to Heaven . . ." and you fill in a way you could go.

The second line gives some reason why you can't get to Heaven that way, and has to rhyme with the last word of the first line.

Here are a few examples:

Oh, you can't get to Heaven _*in a rocking chair*_

'cause _*the Lord don't want no lazy folks there,*_

Oh, you can't get to Heaven _*in a big balloon*_

'cause _*the gosh-darn thing will get stuck on the moon.*_

Try finishing the last line of these:

Oh, you can't get to Heaven _*on a city bus*_

'cause _____ *the smoke and fumes would cause a fuss.*

Oh, you can't get to Heaven _*in a little rowboat*_

'cause _____ *that little boat won't stay afloat.*

Oh, you can't get to Heaven _*in a motor car*_

'cause _____ *there is no gas on the nearest star.*

See if you can make up one of your own.

Oh, you can't get to Heaven _____

'cause _____

Many Meanings

Name_____

Write the word that means both things.

_____ finger-holder; time-teller on a clock

_____ have fun; a stage show

_____*bat*_____ ball-hitter; tiny birdlike mammal

_____ dirty bug; travel through air

_____ something between you and your shoe; to hit

_____ pig-corral; ink-writer

_____ a color; a fruit

_____ car-shoes; wear out

_____ a nonrolling stone; swing a baby

_____ meat-sticker; where the road splits

_____ alphabet-number; mailbox-filler

_____ un-heavy; darkness remover

_____ not smooth road; hit a table

Make up a few of your own. See who can figure them out.

_____ _____

_____ _____

_____ _____

Many Meanings

Name_____

Write the word that means both things.

_____*hand*_____ **finger-holder; time-teller on a clock**

_____*play*_____ **have fun; a stage show**

_____*bat*_____ **ball-hitter; tiny birdlike mammal**

_____*fly*_____ **dirty bug; travel through air**

_____*sock*_____ **something between you and your shoe; to hit**

_____*pen*_____ **pig-corral; ink-writer**

_____*orange*_____ **a color; a fruit**

_____*tire*_____ **car-shoes; wear out**

_____*rock*_____ **a nonrolling stone; swing a baby**

_____*fork*_____ **meat-sticker; where the road splits**

_____*letter*_____ **alphabet-number; mailbox-filler**

_____*light*_____ **un-heavy; darkness remover**

_____*bump*_____ **not smooth road; hit a table**

Make up a few of your own. See who can figure them out.

_____   _____

_____   _____

_____   _____

Descriptive Adjectives

Find someone in the room who fits each of these adjectives. When you and a friend are finished, see if you named the same people.

lanky _____

dainty _____

attractive _____

agile _____

loquacious _____

conscientious _____

sedate _____

gregarious _____

obstreperous _____

affectionate _____

rational _____

unsociable _____

tenacious _____

zany _____

Find a descriptive adjective in the dictionary. _____

Now think of somebody in the room the word describes. Then give the word to a friend, have him look it up. See if he can guess who you were thinking of.

Try it again, this time with two adjectives.

_____   _____

Descriptive Adjectives

Name _____

Find someone in the room who fits each of these adjectives. When you and a friend are finished, see if you named the same people.

lanky _____

dainty _____

attractive _____

agile _____

loquacious _____

conscientious _____

sedate _____

gregarious _____

obstreperous _____

affectionate _____

rational _____

unsociable _____

tenacious _____

zany _____

Find a descriptive adjective in the dictionary. _____

Now think of somebody in the room the word describes. Then give the word to a friend, have him look it up. See if he can guess who you were thinking of.

Try it again, this time with two adjectives.

_____   _____

Treasure Hunt

Name _____

Answer these questions when you know what they mean.

1. **What might an avaricious person do?**

   _____

   _____

2. **If you buy an awl, what might you be making?**

   _____

3. **Where would you cavort?**

   _____

   _____

4. **What subject in school is obnoxious to you?**

   _____

5. **Describe an incredible animal.**

   _____

6. **How far can you expectorate?**

   _____

7. **Name an animal with a large proboscis.**

   _____

8. **When might you prevaricate?**

   _____

9. **What food might make you regurgitate?**

   _____

Treasure Hunt

Name _____

Answer these questions when you know what they mean.

1. **What might an avaricious person do?**

   _____*something to do with*_____

   _____*acquiring money*_____

2. **If you buy an awl, what might you be making?**

   _____*a shoe*_____

3. **Where would you cavort?**

   _____*anywhere you'd have fun,*_____

   _____*a park perhaps*_____

4. **What subject in school is obnoxious to you?**

   _____*any distasteful subject*_____

5. **Describe an incredible animal.**

   _____*monster, dragon, science fiction or fairy tale creature*_____

6. **How far can you expectorate?**

   _____*(distances will vary)*_____

7. **Name an animal with a large proboscis.**

   _____*elephant, elephant seal*_____

8. **When might you prevaricate?**

   _____*in any situation that lying would be the easy way out of*_____

9. **What food might make you regurgitate?**

   _____*any distasteful food*_____

WHAAAAT?

Name _____

Write these sentences in simpler words.

1. The nefarious urchin expectorated.

    _____

2. His elongated proboscis protrudes.

    _____

3. The massive pugilists engaged in fisticuffs.

    _____

4. He prevaricated when his maternal parent interrogated him regarding the missing pralines.

    _____

    _____

5. John slammed the orb over the palisade.

    _____

6. The obnoxious offspring thrust a digit in his sibling's cornea.

    _____

    _____

Write a simple sentence.

_____

Now, look up the important words in a thesaurus, and write the sentence over again using

harder words. _____

_____

Give the hard sentence to somebody else to figure out.

WHAAAAT?

Name _____

Write these sentences in simpler words.

1. **The nefarious urchin expectorated.**

   The bad child spit. _____

2. **His elongated proboscis protrudes.**

   His long nose sticks out. _____

3. **The massive pugilists engaged in fisticuffs.**

   The huge fighters fought. _____

4. **He prevaricated when his maternal parent interrogated him regarding the missing pralines.**

   He lied when his mother asked him about _____

   the missing candy. _____

5. **John slammed the orb over the palisade.**

   John hit the ball over the fence. _____

6. **The obnoxious offspring thrust a digit in his sibling's cornea.**

   The bad child stuck a finger in his (or her) _____

   brother's (or sister's) eye. _____

Write a simple sentence.

_____

Now, look up the important words in a thesaurus, and write the sentence over again using

harder words. _____

_____

Give the hard sentence to somebody else to figure out.

Where Would You Be?

Name _____

1. If you wanted to wink at a wombat, where would you go?

   _____

2. If you saw a bushbaby blush, where would you be?

   _____

3. Who's fussy about fuzz on their fezzes?

   _____

4. Where would you go to see a kob eating corn?

   _____

5. Who would take her sari on a safari?

   _____

6. Where would you ride on a junk?

   _____

7. Where would you go to yack with a yak?

   _____

8. Who would tip his tam-o-shanter at a tourist?

   _____

Find two animals with strange names in the encyclopedia, or in the dictionary. See if other people know where to find them.

_____   _____

Where Would You Be?

Name _____

1. **If you wanted to wink at a wombat, where would you go?**

   Australia or Tasmania

2. **If you saw a bushbaby blush, where would you be?**

   Australia

3. **Who's fussy about fuzz on their fezzes?**

   men in Turkey

4. **Where would you go to see a kob eating corn?**

   Uganda

5. **Who would take her sari on a safari?**

   a woman in India

6. **Where would you ride on a junk?**

   China

7. **Where would you go to yack with a yak?**

   Tibet

8. **Who would tip his tam-o-shanter at a tourist?**

   a man in Scotland

Find two animals with strange names in the encyclopedia, or in the dictionary. See if other people know where to find them.

_____ _____

Sequencing Cartoons

Name _____

Cut these cartoons out and put them in order so they tell a story.

Cut a cartoon series out of a newspaper and give it to somebody else so he or she can try to put it in order.

Sequencing Cartoons

Name _____

Cut these cartoons out and put them in order so they tell a story.

Reprinted by permission of the Chicago Tribune.
Copyright 1973. All rights reserved.

Cut a cartoon series out of a newspaper and give it to somebody else so he or she can try to put it in order.

Sensible Sentences

Name _____

Change the words so they make a sentence.

1. On hunter munched John hungrily alligator the the alligator Fred.

    _____

    _____

2. Clearly chewing one helps on pencils think.

    _____

    _____

3. The the the frightened forest dog through chased huge rabbit.

    _____

    _____

4. Over of be rainbow colors seen could the clouds various.

    _____

    _____

5. Butterflies buds by buzz and beautiful busily bumblebees.

    _____

    _____

Write a sentence of your own. _____

_____

Now, scramble the words in it and write it again. _____

_____

_____ . See who can figure out the scrambled sentence.

Sensible Sentences

Name _____

Change the words so they make a sentence.

1. **On hunter munched John hungrily alligator the the alligator Fred.**

   _____*John the alligator munched hungrily on Fred the*_____

   _____*alligator hunter (or vice-versa).*_____

2. **Clearly chewing one helps on pencils think.**

   _____*Chewing on pencils helps one think clearly.*_____

   _____

3. **The the the frightened forest dog through chased huge rabbit.**

   _____*The huge dog chased the frightened rabbit through*_____

   _____*the forest.*_____

4. **Over of be rainbow colors seen could the clouds various.**

   _____*Over the rainbow could be seen clouds of various*_____

   _____*colors.*_____

5. **Butterflies buds by buzz and beautiful busily bumblebees.**

   _____*Bumblebees buzz busily by beautiful buds and*_____

   _____*butterflies.*_____

Write a sentence of your own. _____

_____

Now, scramble the words in it and write it again. _____

_____

_____ . See who can figure out the scrambled sentence.

Cut-up Article

Name _____

This article has been cut up and put out of order.
Can you cut out the paragraphs and put them back in order?

Approaching the other tower, he could see the policemen waiting for him. They tried to talk to him, but he lay the balancing pole down on the wire, whirled around and picked it up again.

He thought about his walk. He had been gripped by fear, and he fought it. Finally he had laughed at fear, laying down on the wire with his nose in the clouds. He knew the beauty that had surrounded him on that walk would always be with him.

The return trip was complete joy. He felt like a bird—like he belonged to the sky. The wire felt as though it were strung from cloud to cloud.

He stepped carefully, putting one foot in front of another slowly, precisely. The tiptoe touched first, then the sole of the foot slid along the wire. Finally the heel absorbed the full weight of his body.

Breathless with fear he grasped his balancing pole. He set one foot on the wire. The streets below looked like tiny straight rivers at the bottom of a canyon.

He decided to end the walk with a bang. He ran along the wire toward the tower and leaped to the roof. The policemen began clapping and cheering. Two of them grabbed Philippe, but the sergeant said, "Take it easy. This man is an artist."

Cut an interesting article out of the newspaper and cut the paragraphs apart. Tape them to cards so that each paragraph is on a different card.

Then see if somebody can put them in the right order.

Answers:

Cut-up Article

This article has been cut up and put out of order.
Can you cut out the paragraphs and put them back in order?

Approaching the other tower, he could see the policemen waiting for him. They tried to talk to him, but he lay the balancing pole down on the wire, whirled around and picked it up again.

He thought about his walk. He had been gripped by fear, and he fought it. Finally he had laughed at fear, laying down on the wire with his nose in the clouds. He knew the beauty that had surrounded him on that walk would always be with him.

The return trip was complete joy. He felt like a bird—like he belonged to the sky. The wire felt as though it were strung from cloud to cloud.

He stepped carefully, putting one foot in front of another slowly, precisely. The tiptoe touched first, then the sole of the foot slid along the wire. Finally the heel absorbed the full weight of his body.

Breathless with fear he grasped his balancing pole. He set one foot on the wire. The streets below looked like tiny straight rivers at the bottom of a canyon.

He decided to end the walk with a bang. He ran along the wire toward the tower and leaped to the roof. The policemen began clapping and cheering. Two of them grabbed Philippe, but the sergeant said, "Take it easy. This man is an artist."

Cut an interesting article out of the newspaper and cut the paragraphs apart. Tape them to cards so that each paragraph is on a different card.

Then see if somebody can put them in the right order.

Answers: *Breathless with fear . . .*
He stepped carefully . . .
Approaching the other tower . . .
The return trip . . .
He decided to end the walk . . .
He thought about . . .

Word Search

Name _____

Find twelve words that have to do with school.
Write them to the right of the letters.

p	e	n	c	i	l	p	p	q	s	r
x	r	k	s	e	d	q	a	w	s	t
m	a	t	h	e	r	m	l	p	s	e
s	s	f	b	o	o	k	l	l	e	b
w	e	q	c	s	d	u	f	w	c	r
x	r	k	l	a	h	c	o	o	e	g
x	f	r	b	e	t	c	v	n	r	u
d	n	u	o	r	g	y	a	l	p	m
y	m	l	p	p	u	b	x	h	t	o
a	s	z	d	r	i	l	h	s	f	n
r	s	c	i	e	n	c	e	e	y	x
q	t	k	f	j	m	p	t	r	z	g

1. _____

2. _____

3. _____

4. _____

5. _____

6. _____

7. _____

8. _____

9. _____

10. _____

11. _____

12. _____

Make up a word search of your own. Use graph paper. Some topics you might use are: states, cities, colors, football teams, animals, girls' or boys' names.

Word Search

Name _____

Find twelve words that have to do with school.
Write them to the right of the letters.

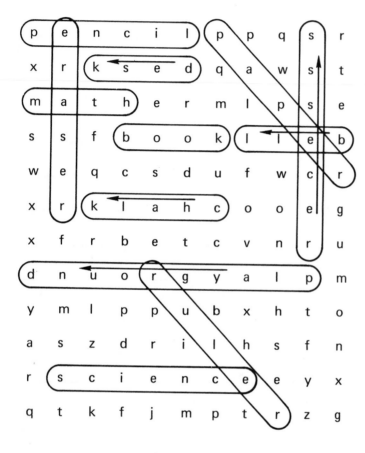

1.	*pencil*
2.	*math*
3.	*science*
4.	*desk*
5.	*eraser*
6.	*paper*
7.	*chalk*
8.	*bell*
9.	*recess*
10.	*playground*
11.	*book*
12.	*ruler*

Make up a word search of your own. Use graph paper. Some topics you might use are:
states, cities, colors, football teams, animals, girls' or boys' names.

Find Them

The name of each of these boys and girls is
hidden in one line below. Can you find
their names?

Al	Ann	Dan
Tim	Susan	Jack
Sam	Ted	Sally
Art	Gay	

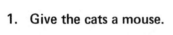

1. Give the cats a mouse.

2. What I might do is dance.

3. See if you can tag a yellow bird.

4. Before you go out, put on your jacket.

5. Hide when a big, red spotted bat comes near!

6. Can nice mice eat rice?

7. Tall ants and green pants fix sick sticks.

8. Do you have another year to wait?

9. Mother gives us an extra cookie when we eat everything.

10. Pass all your papers in when you're finished.

Find Them

The name of each of these boys and girls is hidden in one line below. Can you find their names?

Al	Ann	Dan
Tim	Susan	Jack
Sam	Ted	Sally
Art	Gay	

1. Give the cats a mouse.

2. What I might do is dance.

3. See if you can tag a yellow bird.

4. Before you go out, put on your jacket.

5. Hide when a big, red spotted bat comes near!

6. Can nice mice eat rice?

7. Tall ants and green pants fix sick sticks.

8. Do you have another year to wait?

9. Mother gives us an extra cookie when we eat everything.

10. Pass all your papers in when you're finished.

Hidden Clothing

Name _____

In each sentence below is hidden the name of some simple piece of clothing. Circle each name.

1. Is Ruth at the ball game?

2. The early California padres sent scouts ahead to look for a trail.

3. Does Peg love strawberries and cream?

4. The label tells what is in the can.

5. Jan mows as Tess hoes.

6. Stop ant swallowing—it's not good for you.

7. What I eat is my own business.

8. We had cocoa to warm us up.

9. On the boat, sometimes we ate raw fish.

10. Over all Switzerland, snow fell.

11. Today nine dangerous men tried to hijack Ethiopian Airlines Flight No. 307.

12. The Inca Prince sent his messages by runner.

Does Pe g love strawberries

Make up a couple of your own. Name two pieces of clothing.

_____   _____

Now write two sentences, hiding each piece of clothing somewhere in a sentence. Then give it to somebody.

_____

_____

Hidden Clothing

Name _____

In each sentence below is hidden the name of some simple piece of clothing. Circle each name.

1. Is Ruth at the ball game?

2. The early California padres sent scouts ahead to look for a trail.

3. Does Peg love strawberries and cream?

4. The label tells what is in the can.

5. Jan mows as Tess hoes.

6. Stop ant swallowing—it's not good for you.

7. What I eat is my own business.

8. We had cocoa to warm us up.

9. On the boat, sometimes we ate raw fish.

10. Over all Switzerland, snow fell.

11. Today nine dangerous men tried to hijack Ethiopian Airlines Flight No. 307.

12. The Inca Prince sent his messages by runner.

Does Pe g love strawberries

Make up a couple of your own. Name two pieces of clothing.

_____   _____

Now write two sentences, hiding each piece of clothing somewhere in a sentence. Then give it to somebody.

_____

_____

Word Puzzle

Name _____

1. C any ouf igu reo utt his puz zl e? _____

2. Ma ryw en tt ot hem ov ie. _____

3. Lo okb efo rey oul eap. _____

4. Ra lp hhi tah omer un. _____

5. As ka ndy ouw il lre cei ve. _____

6. Th eco br ac oil edi nab ask et. _____

7. T hean tel op el eap ed. _____

8. Wh ow ont her ace? _____

9. Sa llys eek ssa wto oth edt ig ers. _____

10. Ro be rt run sra pid lyd own th er amp. _____

Make up a sentence of your own. Write it down, then divide the words up.

_____

_____

Now rewrite the sentence in little bits, and give it to someone else to figure out.

_____

_____

Word Puzzle

1. C any ouf igu reo utt his puz zl e? _____ *Can you figure out this puzzle?* _____

2. Ma ryw en tt ot hem ov ie. _____ *Mary went to the movie.* _____

3. Lo okb efo rey oul eap. _____ *Look before you leap.* _____

4. Ra lp hhi tah omer un. _____ *Ralph hit a home run.* _____

5. As ka ndy ouw il lre cei ve. _____ *Ask and you will receive.* _____

6. Th eco br ac oil edi nab ask et. _____ *The cobra coiled in a basket.* _____

7. T hean tel op el eap ed. _____ *The antelope leaped.* _____

8. Wh ow ont her ace? _____ *Who won the race?* _____

9. Sa llys eek ssa wto oth edt ig ers. _____ *Sally seeks sawtoothed tigers.* _____

10. Ro be rt run sra pid lyd own th er amp. _____ *Robert runs rapidly down the ramp.* _____

Make up a sentence of your own. Write it down, then divide the words up.

_____

_____

Now rewrite the sentence in little bits, and give it to someone else to figure out.

_____

_____

Kriss Kross

Name _____

Fit these names into the puzzle above.

Diane	Tom	Sue	Michael
Regina	Carl	Stephanie	Anne
David	Robert	Neil	Ray
Ted	Ronald	Al	Gregory
Cindy	George	Elizabeth	Donna
Nancy	Kim	Carol	Mary

Make up a Kriss Kross. Use school words, the names of people in your class, streets, schools, animals, or the names of teams or cars in your Kriss Kross.

Kriss Kross

Name _____

Fit these names into the puzzle above.

Diane	**Tom**	**Sue**	**Michael**
Regina	**Carl**	**Stephanie**	**Anne**
David	**Robert**	**Neil**	**Ray**
Ted	**Ronald**	**Al**	**Gregory**
Cindy	**George**	**Elizabeth**	**Donna**
Nancy	**Kim**	**Carol**	**Mary**

Make up a Kriss Kross. Use school words, the names of people in your class, streets, schools, animals, or the names of teams or cars in your Kriss Kross.

Copyright © 1975 by Addison-Wesley Publishing Company, Inc.

16

CROSSES

Name _____

Crosses is a game you can play with a friend, or with a couple of friends.

Print any letter you like in each star.

At the beginning of each line, print the name of a group of things, such as sports, flowers, TV shows, colors, or anything else you like.

Then see if you can fill all the boxes with the name of something that should be in that row, and that begins with the letter on top.

We did one to show you.

	☆ B	☆ S	☆ T
animals	bear	skunk	tiger
names	Bob	Sue	Tom
sports	baseball	swimming	tennis

Try doing this one.

	☆ R	☆ T
plants		
colors		
food		

Now make up one of your own.

	☆	☆

Here are some other groups you might try:

trees, boys' or girls' names, states, movies, kind of dogs, toys, games, food.

CROSSES

Name _____

Crosses is a game you can play with a friend, or with a couple of friends.

Print any letter you like in each star.

At the beginning of each line, print the name of a group of things, such as sports, flowers, TV shows, colors, or anything else you like.

Then see if you can fill all the boxes with the name of something that should be in that row, and that begins with the letter on top.

We did one to show you.

	⭐B	⭐S	⭐T
animals	bear	skunk	tiger
names	Bob	Sue	Tom
sports	baseball	swimming	tennis

Try doing this one.

	⭐R	⭐T
plants		
colors		
food		

Now make up one of your own.

	⭐	⭐

Here are some other groups you might try:

trees, boys' or girls' names, states, movies, kind of dogs, toys, games, food.

Categories

This is a game you can play with one or more of your friends.

At the top of each column, write a letter.

Beside each row, name a category such as foods, airplanes, states, animals, or anything else.

The first person to fill in all the boxes on his sheet wins. Each box is filled with the name of something in the category that begins with the letter at the top of the row.

The one below has been started for you — try to finish it.

	T	S	R	P
animals		snake	rat	
clothing	top coat	scarf	rain coat	
girls' names		Sue		Paula
cars				Pontiac

Make up one of your own, and challenge somebody!

Some categories you might try are: tools, parts of the body, trees, kinds of dogs, book titles, countries, feelings, vehicles, or anything you want.

Categories

This is a game you can play with one or more of your friends.

At the top of each column, write a letter.

Beside each row, name a category such as foods, airplanes, states, animals, or anything else.

The first person to fill in all the boxes on his sheet wins. Each box is filled with the name of something in the category that begins with the letter at the top of the row.

The one below has been started for you — try to finish it.

	T	S	R	P
animals		snake	rat	
clothing	top coat	scarf	rain coat	
girls' names		Sue		Paula
cars				Pontiac

Make up one of your own, and challenge somebody!

Some categories you might try are: tools, parts of the body, trees, kinds of dogs, book titles, countries, feelings, vehicles, or anything you want.

Word Lists

Name _____

Put all the words in heavy type in four lists of the same kinds of things.

fog	**helicopter**	**thunder**	**clouds**	**raincoat**	**turquoise**	**bat**
green	**red**	**eagle**	**sweater**	**airplane**	**shirt**	**black**
jeans	**cap**	**bee**	**blue**	**rain**	**sunshine**	

_____   _____   _____   _____

_____   _____   _____   _____

_____   _____   _____   _____

_____   _____   _____   _____

_____   _____   _____   _____

_____   _____   _____   _____

Make up four lists of things. At the top of each list, write what kinds of things they are.

_____   _____   _____   _____

_____   _____   _____   _____

_____   _____   _____   _____

_____   _____   _____   _____

_____   _____   _____   _____

_____   _____   _____   _____

Now, scramble up the words as you write them again. Make sure you don't include the words that tell what kind of things there are in each list.

Give the list of scrambled words to somebody else to see if the person can put them in four categories.

_____   _____   _____   _____

_____   _____   _____   _____

_____   _____   _____   _____

_____   _____   _____   _____

_____   _____   _____   _____

Word Lists

Name _____

Put all the words in heavy type in four lists of the same kinds of things.

fog   **helicopter**   **thunder**   **clouds**   **raincoat**   **turquoise**   **bat**
green   **red**   **eagle**   **sweater**   **airplane**   **shirt**   **black**
jeans   **cap**   **bee**   **blue**   **rain**   **sunshine**

(Colors)	*(Clothing)*	*(Weather)*	*(Flying Things)*
red	*cap*	*thunder*	*eagle*
black	*shirt*	*sunshine*	*bat*
green	*jeans*	*fog*	*helicopter*
turquoise	*raincoat*	*rain*	*airplane*
blue	*sweater*	*clouds*	*bee*

Make up four lists of things. At the top of each list, write what kinds of things they are.

Now, scramble up the words as you write them again. Make sure you don't include the words that tell what kind of things there are in each list.

Give the list of scrambled words to somebody else to see if the person can put them in four categories.

Cookbook

Name _____

You can see the headings on the cookbook below.

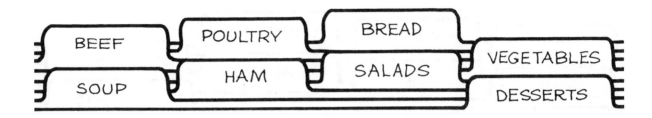

Where would you look up the recipe for these things?

chicken _____   ham _____

baked beans _____   tomato soup _____

applesauce _____   dumplings _____

steak _____   turkey _____

orange angel food cake _____   apple pie _____

cole slaw _____

Make a list of some of the things you'd like to have for a feast.

_____   _____

_____   _____

_____   _____

_____   _____

See if somebody else can find them in a cookbook for you.

Cookbook

You can see the headings on the cookbook below.

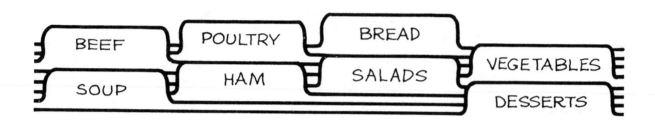

Where would you look up the recipe for these things?

chicken	_poultry_	**ham**	_ham_
baked beans	_vegetables_	**tomato soup**	_soup_
applesauce	_desserts_	**dumplings**	_bread_
steak	_beef_	**turkey**	_poultry_
orange angel food cake	_desserts_	**apple pie**	_desserts_
cole slaw	_salads_		

Make a list of some of the things you'd like to have for a feast.

_____   _____

_____   _____

_____   _____

_____   _____

See if somebody else can find them in a cookbook for you.

Want Ads

Name _____

The index tells you what section of the want ads to look something up in.

Here is the index:

WANT AD INDEX

ANNOUNCEMENTS
Business Notices 31
Home Service 85
Legal Notices 895
Lost and Found 15
Moving and Storage 65
Personals 30
Public Notices 25
Tours-Travel 75
Transportation 70

AUTOMOTIVE
Autos, New, Used 430
Autos, Wanted 425
Hot Rod Column 440
Collectors' Cars 445
Imported and Sports Cars 435
Motorcycles and Scooters 420
Trucks-Equipment. 405
Campers-Trailers 410

BOATS AND AIRPLANES
Airplanes & Flying 180
Boats & Boating 175

BUSINESS OFFERS
Business For Sale 600
Motels For Sale 605
Mobile Parks For Sale . . 610

EDUCATIONAL
Instruction 190
Music Instruction 130

EMPLOYMENT
Jobs Offered
Household Help 310
Help Wanted 333
Couples 333-1
Temporary 333-2
Agencies 333-3
Career Aids 195

Jobs Wanted
Jobs Wanted, Women . . . 200
Jobs Wanted 205
Jobs Wanted, Men 210

FINANCIAL
Money Loaned &
    Wanted 40 40-1
Real Estate Loans . 700 700-1

MERCHANDISE
Antiques, Art 110
Photography 135
Contractors Machinery
    Heavy Equipment 160
Diamonds, Gold Jewelry . 100
Furnishings,
    Appliances 115-120
Furs 100
Hi Fi, Radio, TV. 125
Machinery. 155
Musical Instruments 130
Miscellaneous 100
Office Furniture Sup-
    plies, Typewriters 140
Printers Column 165

PETS
Dogs, Cats, Birds,
    Fish, etc. 145
Stud Service 145
Horses, Livestock,
    Farm Equipment 150

REAL ESTATE
Community Apartments . 720
Country Property 770
Homes for Sale 730-750
Income Property. 755
Industrial and Business 760-765
Bay Area Lots 710
Real Estate to Exchange
    and Wanted 775-780
Mobile Homes, Parks . . . 885

RENTALS
Apts., Flats, Duplexes,
    Homes 545-565
Suburban Rentals . . 570-580
Business 590
Hotels, Motels 520
Rooms 525
Rentals, Wanted 500
Rest Homes 505
Vacation Rentals 585

SPORTS
See Sportman's Corner
in Sports Section

What numbers would you find these things under?

a house _____

a used pickup truck? _____

a bicycle _____

somebody to haul trash _____

a camera _____

an apartment to rent _____

your lost dog _____

a used TV _____

a summer job _____

a washing machine _____

Cut out the index to your newspaper's want ads, and tape it to a piece of paper.

Then look for ads that are different, and write them down.

See if other people can figure out what section they came from.

Want Ads

Name _____

The index tells you what section of the want ads to look something up in.

Here is the index:

WANT AD INDEX

ANNOUNCEMENTS
Business Notices 31
Home Service 85
Legal Notices 895
Lost and Found 15
Moving and Storage 65
Personals 30
Public Notices 25
Tours-Travel 75
Transportation 70

AUTOMOTIVE
Autos, New, Used 430
Autos, Wanted 425
Hot Rod Column 440
Collectors' Cars 445
Imported and Sports Cars 435
Motorcycles and Scooters 420
Trucks-Equipment. 405
Campers-Trailers 410

BOATS AND AIRPLANES
Airplanes & Flying 180
Boats & Boating 175

BUSINESS OFFERS
Business For Sale 600
Motels For Sale 605
Mobile Parks For Sale . . 610

EDUCATIONAL
Instruction 190
Music Instruction 130

EMPLOYMENT
Jobs Offered
Household Help 310
Help Wanted 333
Couples 333-1
Temporary 333-2
Agencies 333-3
Career Aids 195

Jobs Wanted
Jobs Wanted, Women . . . 200
Jobs Wanted 205
Jobs Wanted, Men 210

FINANCIAL
Money Loaned &
   Wanted 40 40-1
Real Estate Loans . 700 700-1

MERCHANDISE
Antiques, Art 110
Photography 135
Contractors Machinery
   Heavy Equipment 160
Diamonds, Gold Jewelry . 100
Furnishings,
   Appliances 115-120
Furs 100
Hi Fi, Radio, TV. 125
Machinery. 155
Musical Instruments 130
Miscellaneous 100
Office Furniture Sup-
   plies, Typewriters 140
Printers Column 165

PETS
Dogs, Cats, Birds,
   Fish, etc. 145
Stud Service 145
Horses, Livestock,
   Farm Equipment 150

REAL ESTATE
Community Apartments . 720
Country Property 770
Homes for Sale 730-750
Income Property. 755
Industrial and Business760-765
Bay Area Lots 710
Real Estate to Exchange
   and Wanted 775-780
Mobile Homes, Parks . . . 885

RENTALS
Apts., Flats, Duplexes,
   Homes 545-565
Suburban Rentals . . 570-580
Business 590
Hotels, Motels 520
Rooms 525
Rentals, Wanted 500
Rest Homes 505
Vacation Rentals 585

SPORTS
See Sportman's Corner
in Sports Section

What numbers would you find these things under?

a house _____ *730-750*

a used pickup truck? _____ *430*

a bicycle _____ *100*

somebody to haul trash _____ *65*

a camera _____ *135*

an apartment to rent _____ *545-565*

your lost dog _____ *15*

a used TV _____ *125*

a summer job _____ *333*

a washing machine _____ *115-120*

Cut out the index to your newspaper's want ads, and tape it to a piece of paper.

Then look for ads that are different, and write them down.

See if other people can figure out what section they came from.

Telephone Book

Name _____

Use the index in your telephone book to find these things in the yellow pages:

Main Heading You'd Look Up

kites _____

gas stations _____

cribs _____

piano lessons _____

sleds _____

puppies _____

saddles _____

airplane tickets _____

minibikes _____

baseball tickets _____

private detectives _____

doctors _____

Write down some things you'd like to find out where to get or buy. See if somebody else can find them for you in the yellow pages' index.

THINGS	WHERE TO LOOK
_____	_____
_____	_____
_____	_____

Telephone Book

Name _____

Use the index in your telephone book to find these things in the yellow pages:

Main Heading You'd Look Up

kites _____ *toy stores* _____

gas stations _____ *service stations* _____

cribs _____ *infant furniture* _____

piano lessons _____ *instruction* _____

sleds _____ *sporting goods* _____

puppies _____ *pets, dogs* _____

saddles _____ *horseman's equipment* _____

airplane tickets _____ *air travel* _____

minibikes _____ *motorcycles* _____

baseball tickets _____ *theatre and sports tickets* _____

private detectives _____ *investigators* _____

doctors _____ *physicians* _____

Write down some things you'd like to find out where to get or buy. See if somebody else can find them for you in the yellow pages' index.

THINGS   WHERE TO LOOK

_____   _____

_____   _____

_____   _____

Nonsense Words in Sentences

Name _____

Figure out what each nonsense word means. Then write it above the word.

1. Frangling at school will get you in trouble.

2. John had a hole in his zitch, and his boof got wet.

3. Susan tied a longer lurb to her keepong, so it would sarm better.

4. The arp became frip, and it began to plardol.

5. When you put a gowrf on top of a shlegel, it usually poweles.

6. From inside the bilox, you could see the langet sworbly.

7. Mary filled a scla so pogley that it hadled.

8. In the early morning light, she could hardly see the zorab in front of the pilastrom.

Make up a few nonsense sentences of your own, and see who can figure them out.

Nonsense Words in Sentences   Name _____

Figure out what each nonsense word means. Then write it above the word.

     (Fighting)
1.   Frangling at school will get you in trouble.

              (shoe)   *(sock)*
2.   John had a hole in his zitch, and his boof got wet.

              (tail)   *(kite)*   *(fly)*
3.   Susan tied a longer lurb to her keepong, so it would sarm better.

4.   The arp became frip, and it began to plardol.

5.   When you put a gowrf on top of a shlegel, it usually poweles.

6.   From inside the bilox, you could see the langet sworbly.

             (glass) *(full)*   *(spilled)*
7.   Mary filled a scla so pogley that it hadled.

                            (moose)   *(cabin)*
8.   In the early morning light, she could hardly see the zorab in front of the pilastrom.

(These are just suggested answers; many others are possible.)

Make up a few nonsense sentences of your own, and see who can figure them out.

Nonsense Words in a Story

Name _____

Read the following story. There are some nonsense words in it that you should be able to figure out from the rest of the story. At the end of the story, circle the correct meanings of the nonsense words.

A fox, a bear, and a wolf were walking along beside the river. The bear saw a fine fat fish in the water. He reached down with his large paw and <u>sworf</u> the fish out onto the bank. Quickly the wolf jumped on the fish and <u>prend</u> it so that it couldn't slip back into the water.

"Get away from my fish," said the bear.

"I should get part of it," cried the wolf. "Because I kept the fish from slipping back into the <u>aquare</u>."

"Let me settle this," said the fox. "There's no need for you to <u>bracht</u>.

"The bear saw the fish first, so he should get the head," and the fox gave the head to the bear.

"The <u>lupe</u> then held the fish. He should get the tail," and the fox gave the <u>finit</u> to the wolf.

Then the fox quickly ate the rest of the <u>icthis</u> himself. He said, "And I get the body for <u>essing</u> the judge."

1.	<u>sworf</u> means	ate	looked	knocked	held
2.	<u>prend</u> means	watched	held	wolf	toy
3.	<u>aquare</u> means	swim	river	bank	fish
4.	<u>bracht</u> means	fight	fish	look	be
5.	<u>lupe</u> means	fight	fox	pole	wolf
6.	<u>finit</u> means	meat	eye	tail	throat
7.	<u>icthis</u> means	head	fish	river	fox
8.	<u>essing</u> means	being	shooting	knocking	fighting

Make up your own Context Clues story by rewriting a very short story with a few nonsense words in place of regular words.

List the nonsense words under the story and give four choices. See who can get them all right.

Nonsense Words in a Story

Name _____

Read the following story. There are some nonsense words in it that you should be able to figure out from the rest of the story. At the end of the story, circle the correct meanings of the nonsense words.

A fox, a bear, and a wolf were walking along beside the river. The bear saw a fine fat fish in the water. He reached down with his large paw and <u>sworf</u> the fish out onto the bank. Quickly the wolf jumped on the fish and <u>prend</u> it so that it couldn't slip back into the water.

"Get away from my fish," said the bear.

"I should get part of it," cried the wolf. "Because I kept the fish from slipping back into the <u>aquare</u>."

"Let me settle this," said the fox. "There's no need for you to <u>bracht</u>.

"The bear saw the fish first, so he should get the head," and the fox gave the head to the bear.

"The <u>lupe</u> then held the fish. He should get the tail," and the fox gave the <u>finit</u> to the wolf.

Then the fox quickly ate the rest of the <u>icthis</u> himself. He said, "And I get the body for <u>essing</u> the judge."

1.	<u>sworf</u> means	ate	looked	(knocked)	held
2.	<u>prend</u> means	watched	(held)	wolf	toy
3.	<u>aquare</u> means	swim	(river)	bank	fish
4.	<u>bracht</u> means	(fight)	fish	look	be
5.	<u>lupe</u> means	fight	(fox)	pole	wolf
6.	<u>finit</u> means	meat	eye	(tail)	throat
7.	<u>icthis</u> means	head	(fish)	river	fox
8.	<u>essing</u> means	(being)	shooting	knocking	fighting

Make up your own Context Clues story by rewriting a very short story with a few nonsense words in place of regular words.

List the nonsense words under the story and give four choices. See who can get them all right.

Add-a-Letter

Name _____

The word that belongs in the second blank is made up of the word that belongs in the first blank plus one letter.

1. He took his _____ for a ride in

   the _____ .

   YOU DRAW THE PICTURE!

2. Carol got a better _____ this summer

   _____ last summer.

3. We _____ dinner _____ last night.

4. Did your mom _____ say you could

   _____ out late to play?

5. Brush off the _____ before you

   _____ in the shower.

6. Maggie was _____ when her friend _____ bad things about her.

7. They ate the ___*pie*___ under the ___*pine*___ tree.

8. When you find _____ rocks, _____ you're finished.

9. _____ the children wanted the _____ to play with.

10. The boys bought wood _____ building a _____ .

Make up one of your own. Write two words by adding a letter to one of them to make the other.

_____   _____

Leave them blank in a sentence. See who can do it.

_____

_____

Add-a-Letter

Name _____

The word that belongs in the second blank is made up of the word that belongs in the first blank plus one letter.

1. He took his ___cat___ for a ride in

   the___cart___ .

YOU DRAW THE PICTURE!

2. Carol got a better___tan___ this summer

   ___than___ last summer.

3. We___ate___ dinner___late___ last night.

4. Did your mom ___say___ say you could

   ___stay___ out late to play?

5. Brush off the___sand___ before you

   ___stand___ in the shower.

6. Maggie was ___sad___ when her friend___said___ bad things about her.

7. They ate the___pie___ under the___pine___ tree.

8. When you find ___ten___ rocks, ___then___ you're finished.

9. ___All___ the children wanted the ___ball___ to play with.

10. The boys bought wood ___for___ building a ___fort___ .

Make up one of your own. Write two words by adding a letter to one of them to make the other.

_____   _____

Leave them blank in a sentence. See who can do it.

_____

_____

Reading Choices

Name _____

Directions: Choose the correct answer for each question. Circle the letter of the correct answer.

1. James went to town:
   a. there was a box   b. turtle walked past   c. to get bread

2. How did James go?
   a. to get bread   b. by car   c. at 5 o'clock

3. Where has Sam gone?
   a. to the ball park   b. this afternoon   c. with Johnny

4. What was Jeremy holding?
   a. 4 o'clock   b. fourth can   c. some ketchup

5. Which two people won the game?
   a. the taller ones   b. in the back yard   c. by playing hard

6. When did the accident happen?
   a. on Clark Street   b. at noon   c. the blue car

7. Who won the game?
   a. Gordon   b. at 3 o'clock   c. because he kicks well

8. How did Mary Ann write?
   a. during spelling   b. quickly   c. she was smart

Make up some who, what, why questions of your own. Have someone else figure out the answers.

Reading Choices

Name _____

Directions: Choose the correct answer for each question. Circle the letter of the correct answer.

1. James went to town:
   a. there was a box
   b. turtle walked past
   (c.) to get bread

2. How did James go?
   a. to get bread
   (b.) by car
   c. at 5 o'clock

3. Where has Sam gone?
   (a.) to the ball park
   b. this afternoon
   c. with Johnny

4. What was Jeremy holding?
   a. 4 o'clock
   b. fourth can
   (c.) some ketchup

5. Which two people won the game?
   (a.) the taller ones
   b. in the back yard
   c. by playing hard

6. When did the accident happen?
   a. on Clark Street
   (b.) at noon
   c. the blue car

7. Who won the game?
   (a.) Gordon
   b. at 3 o'clock
   c. because he kicks well

8. How did Mary Ann write?
   a. during spelling
   (b.) quickly
   c. she was smart

Make up some who, what, why questions of your own. Have someone else figure out the answers.

Answers to Write Questions for Name _____

On this page, we wrote the answers,
so you write the questions.

1. _____

   _____

   _____

   answer: **When the seagull flew into the rainbow.**

2. _____

   _____

   _____

   answer: **Because she couldn't get any more in without squashing them.**

3. _____

   _____

   answer: **Over the trees whenever it rains.**

4. *Who found the pearl in the grass*
   for the prince?

   answer: **The kindest ant in the anthill.**

5. _____

   _____

   answer: **Just before the big wind came and blew the glass out of all the windows.**

6. _____

   _____

   answer: **With three of his friends and a dog to keep watch.**

Write your own answer: _____

_____

Give it to a friend to make up a question for.

Answers to Write Questions for Name _____

On this page, we wrote the answers,
so you write the questions.

1. _____

   _____

   _____

   answer: When the seagull flew into the rainbow.

2. _____

   _____

   _____

   answer: Because she couldn't get any more in without squashing them.

3. _____

   _____

   answer: Over the trees whenever it rains.

4. *Who found the pearl in the grass for the prince?*

   answer: The kindest ant in the anthill.

5. _____

   _____

   answer: Just before the big wind came and blew the glass out of all the windows.

6. _____

   _____

   answer: With three of his friends and a dog to keep watch.

Write your own answer: _____

_____

Give it to a friend to make up a question for.

GoFer

Write the root word for each of the following words.

unhappiness _____

dissatisfaction _____

impatiently _____

fearlessly _____

undesirable _____

discontented _____

antidisestablishmentarianism _____

misbehavior _____

repayment _____

unlikely _____

transcontinental _____

disorganized _____

unpresentable _____

Make up three of your own. Think of common words, then add as many prefixes and suffixes to them as you can.

_____

_____

_____

GoFer

Write the root word for each of the following words.

unhappiness _____ *happy* _____

dissatisfaction _____ *satisfy* _____

impatiently _____ *patient* _____

fearlessly _____ *fear* _____

undesirable _____ *desire* _____

discontented _____ *content* _____

antidisestablishmentarianism _____ *establish*

misbehavior _____ *behave* _____

repayment _____ *pay* _____

unlikely _____ *like* _____

transcontinental _____ *continent* _____

disorganized _____ *organize* _____

unpresentable _____ *present* _____

Make up three of your own. Think of common words, then add as many prefixes and suffixes to them as you can.

_____

_____

_____

PREfix

Name _____

Fill in the rest of the word

con _____ is care

con _____ is a musical show

con _____*crete*_____ is cement

con _____ is a big bird

con _____ is a musical leader

con _____ is candy

con _____ is tiny pieces of paper to throw

con _____ is to mix up

con _____ is to bring together

con _____ is to defeat

con _____ is to save

con _____ is a group of stars

con _____ is to keep going

Make up a set of your own. You might try these prefixes:

un-   ,   dis-   ,   re-   ,   pre-   ,   tele-   .

PREfix

Name _____

Fill in the rest of the word

con ___*cern*___ is care

con ___*cert*___ is a musical show

con ___*crete*___ is cement

con ___*dor*___ is a big bird

con ___*ductor*___ is a musical leader

con ___*fection*___ is candy

con ___*fetti*___ is tiny pieces of paper to throw

con ___*fuse*___ is to mix up

con ___*geal*___ is to bring together

con ___*quer*___ is to defeat

con ___*serve*___ is to save

con ___*stellation*___ is a group of stars

con ___*tinue*___ is to keep going

Make up a set of your own. You might try these prefixes:

un- , dis- , re- , pre- , tele- .

PRE- and SUF-fixes

Name _____

Fill in the rest of the word.

A_____ less person breaks things.

A_____ less person is lonely.

A_____ less tablecloth is clean.

A_____ less person never says thanks.

A_____*friend*_____ ly person is nice to you.

A_____ ly person is beautiful.

Make no noise; do it _____ ly.

Don't let anyone know; do it _____ly.

Be smart; do it _____ ly.

Try some of your own. Give them to a friend to figure out.

PRE- and SUF-fixes

Name _____

Fill in the rest of the word.

A_____*care*_____ less person breaks things.

A_____*friend*_____ less person is lonely.

A_____*spot*_____ less tablecloth is clean.

A_____*thank*_____ less person never says thanks.

A_____*friend*_____ ly person is nice to you.

A_____*love*_____ ly person is beautiful.

Make no noise; do it _____*quiet*_____ ly.

Don't let anyone know; do it _____*secret*_____ ly.

Be smart; do it _____*correct*_____ ly.

Try some of your own. Give them to a friend to figure out.

Cutoffs

Name _____

you've heard of a disgruntled teacher—
   what would a gruntled teacher be?

_____

if you've ever heard of a disaster—
   what's an aster?

_____

everybody can pretend—
   but can they tend?

_____

a person can respond to a letter—
   but how would he spond?

_____

HE SURELY
LOOKS GUSTED
TODAY.

What would these mean?

spire (as in inspire) _____

hausted (as in exhausted) _____

trieve (as in retrieve) _____

gusted (as in disgusted) _____

Make up a few of your own—and see if somebody can figure them out.

_____ (as in _____)

_____ (as in _____)

Cutoffs

you've heard of a disgruntled teacher—
   what would a gruntled teacher be?

_____ *pleased* _____

if you've ever heard of a disaster—
   what's an aster?

_____ *a happy event* _____

These answers are just examples. Other answers are acceptable.

everybody can pretend—
   but can they tend?

_____ *be honest* _____

a person can respond to a letter—
   but how would he spond?

_____ *write originally* _____

HE SURELY LOOKS GUSTED TODAY.

What would these mean?

spire (as in inspire) _____ *breathe* _____

hausted (as in exhausted) _____ *spirited* _____

trieve (as in retrieve) _____ *carry* _____

gusted (as in disgusted) _____ *enthused* _____

Make up a few of your own—and see if somebody can figure them out.

_____ (as in _____)

_____ (as in _____)

Noords

Name _____

Write down a guess at what these words mean.

zitch — _____

untree — _____

appleful — _____

windsome — _____

betoe — _____

disglow — _____

geeing — _____

frangle — _____

prewith — _____

dislook — _____

Make up some of your own words. Write their meanings on another paper. Let other people guess what your words mean.

_____ — _____

_____ — _____

Noords

Name _____

Write down a guess at what these words mean.

*Any answer that shows
creativity and some cognizance
of the prefix or suffix will do.*

zitch — _____

untree — _____

appleful — _____

windsome — _____

betoe — _____

disglow — _____

geeing — _____

frangle — _____

prewith — _____

dislook — _____

Make up some of your own words. Write their meanings on another paper. Let other people guess what your words mean.

_____ — _____

_____ — _____

Word Compounds

Name _____

🧺	+	🏐	= _____
🌷	+	🫖	= _____
🫘	+	🛍️	= _____
📄	+	😊	= _____
	+		= _____
🌳	+	🪀	= _____
	+		= _____
	+	🍽️	= _____

Make up some drawings of compound words of your own. Give them to a friend to figure out.

Word Compounds

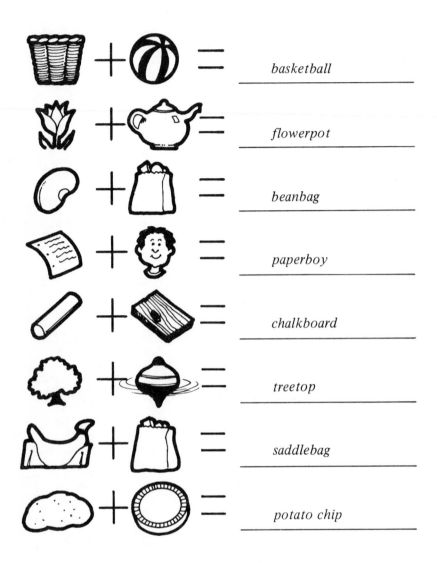

basketball _____

flowerpot _____

beanbag _____

paperboy _____

chalkboard _____

treetop _____

saddlebag _____

potato chip _____

Make up some drawings of compound words of your own. Give them to a friend to figure out.

Togetherness

Write a compound word suggested by these words.

boot tie   _____

colorless hat   _____

digit spike   *fingernail*

hot spot   _____

power ship   _____

shore sphere   _____

liquid drop   _____

fun earth   _____

joint hat   _____

auto haven   _____

cranium hurt   _____

LIQUID DROP

Make up a few of your own. Write down two compound words.

1. _____   2. _____

Now think of some other words that mean the same as the two parts of the compound words.
Then give them to a friend to see if they can figure out the words.

1. _____   _____

2. _____   _____

Togetherness

Name _____

Write a compound word suggested by these words.

boot tie	_shoelace_
colorless hat	_whitecap_
digit spike	*fingernail*
hot spot	_fireplace_
power ship	_motorboat_
shore sphere	_beachball_
liquid drop	_waterfall_
fun earth	_playground_
joint hat	_kneecap_
auto haven	_carport_
cranium hurt	_headache_

LIQUID DROP

Make up a few of your own. Write down two compound words.

1. _____   2. _____

Now think of some other words that mean the same as the two parts of the compound words.
Then give them to a friend to see if they can figure out the words.

1. _____   _____

2. _____   _____

Fill in the Blanks

Name _____

___ in — what you stick in a balloon to pop it

___ in — what a fish uses to swim with

___ in — what you like to do when you play a game

___ ___ in — what you do with a top

___ ___ in — what you wash when you take a bath

___ in ___ — what you have to do when you've lost something

___ in ___ — what you need when you can't get the answer

___ in ___ — what you do with a song

___ in ___ — what you draw with a ruler

___ in ___ ___ ___ — what you eat at night

___ an — what your father is

___ an ___ — what you put in a glove

___ an ___ — what you find at the beach

___ an ___ — where you keep money

___ ___ an — what you get when you need money

___ an — what you fry hamburgers in

___ an ___ — what you wave to make magic

___ an ___ ___ ___ — what you pull to get in a car

___ ___ an ___ — what you do when you don't want to sit

___ ___ an — how you feel when you're angry

_g_ _r_ in

Make up a couple for a friend to try.

___ ___ ___ ___ ___   _____

___ ___ ___ ___ ___   _____

___ ___ ___ ___ ___   _____

___ ___ ___ ___ ___   _____

Fill in the Blanks

Name _____

_<u>p</u>_ in   what you stick in a balloon
to pop it

_<u>f</u>_ in   what a fish uses to swim with

_<u>w</u>_ in   what you like to do when you
play a game

_<u>s</u>_ _<u>p</u>_ in   what you do with a top

_<u>s</u>_ _<u>k</u>_ in   what you wash when you take a bath

_<u>f</u>_ in _<u>d</u>_   what you have to do when you've lost something

_<u>h</u>_ in _<u>t</u>_   what you need when you can't get the answer

_<u>s</u>_ in _<u>g</u>_   what you do with a song

_<u>l</u>_ in _<u>e</u>_   what you draw with a ruler

_<u>d</u>_ in _<u>n</u>_ _<u>e</u>_ _<u>r</u>_   what you eat at night

_<u>m</u>_ an   what your father is

_<u>h</u>_ an _<u>d</u>_   what you put in a glove

_<u>s</u>_ an _<u>d</u>_   what you find at the beach

_<u>b</u>_ an _<u>k</u>_   where you keep money   _<u>g</u>_ _<u>r</u>_ in

_<u>l</u>_ _<u>o</u>_ an   what you get when you need money

_<u>p</u>_ an   what you fry hamburgers in

_<u>w</u>_ an _<u>d</u>_   what you wave to make magic

_<u>h</u>_ an _<u>d</u>_ _<u>l</u>_ _<u>e</u>_   what you pull to get in a car

_<u>s</u>_ _<u>t</u>_ an _<u>d</u>_   what you do when you don't want to sit

_<u>m</u>_ _<u>e</u>_ an   how you feel when you're angry

Make up a couple for a friend to try.

— — — — —   _____

— — — — —   _____

— — — — —   _____

— — — — —   _____

More Add-a-Letter

Name _____

Add the same letter to each word in a line to make it a new word.
Write the new word beside it.

f	l	t
lie _____ *life* _____	sight _____	sand _____
at _____ *fat* _____	fight _____	able _____
lit _____	oaf _____	an _____
let _____	caves _____	in _____
lea _____	save _____	rough _____
lying _____	sat _____	boa _____
ell _____	bow _____	seal _____

See if you can figure out which letter to add to each of these word lines.
Write the new word beside the line.

_____	_____	_____
tie _____	love _____	and _____
sell _____	low _____	eight _____
cap _____	sin _____	sing _____
cob _____	rate _____	on _____
all _____	bride _____	seat _____
lab _____	lee _____	sell _____
site _____	ride _____	hat _____

Try making up several words of your own that have the same missing letter.
Give them to a friend to figure out.

_____ _____ _____ _____

_____ _____ _____ _____

_____ _____ _____ _____

More Add-a-Letter

Name _____

Add the same letter to each word in a line to make it a new word.
Write the new word beside it.

	f			**l**			**t**
lie	*life*		sight	*slight*		sand	*stand*
at	*fat*		fight	*flight*		able	*table*
lit	*flit/lift*		oaf	*loaf*		an	*tan/ant*
let	*left*		caves	*calves*		in	*tin*
lea	*leaf/flea*		save	*slave/salve*		rough	*trough*
lying	*flying*		sat	*salt/slat*		boa	*boat*
ell	*fell*		bow	*blow/bowl*		seal	*steal*

See if you can figure out which letter to add to each of these word lines.
Write the new word beside the line.

	m			**g**			**w**
tie	*time*		love	*glove*		and	*wand*
sell	*smell*		low	*glow*		eight	*weight*
cap	*camp*		sin	*sing/sign*		sing	*swing*
cob	*comb*		rate	*grate*		on	*won/own*
all	*mall*		bride	*bridge*		seat	*sweat*
lab	*lamb*		lee	*glee*		sell	*swell*
site	*smite*		ride	*ridge*		hat	*what*

Try making up several words of your own that have the same missing letter.
Give them to a friend to figure out.

_____ _____ _____ _____

_____ _____ _____ _____

_____ _____ _____ _____

Add-a-Letter Sentences

Name _____

Add the big letter to some words in the sentence, so that the sentence makes sense.

R   The at ate bead and wate.

_____

N   Bed the arrow box eatly.

_____

T   Do no sand on he able.

_____

D   ay is one with inner.

_____

C   arol's ute at was aught under the ot.

_____

R   The ed bid flew though the foest.

_____

Make up a sentence that has at least three words with the same letter in them. Write it.

_____

_____

Now write the sentence again, but leave out one letter every time it appears in a word.

_____

_____

Give the sentence with missing letters to someone else and see if she or he can figure out what it means.

Add-a-Letter Sentences

Name _____

Add the big letter to some words in the sentence, so that the sentence makes sense.

R   The ^{r}at ate ^{r}bead and wate^r.

_____

N   Be^{n}d the ^{n}arrow box ^{n}eatly.

_____

T   Do no^t ^{t}sand on ^{t}he ^{t}able.

_____

D ^{D}ay is ^{d}one with ^{d}inner.

_____

C ^{C}arol's ^{c}ute ^{c}at was ^{c}aught under the ^{c}ot.

_____

R   The ^{r}ed bi^{r}d flew ^{r}though the fo^{r}est.

_____

Make up a sentence that has at least three words with the same letter in them. Write it.

_____

_____

Now write the sentence again, but leave out one letter every time it appears in a word.

_____

_____

Give the sentence with missing letters to someone else and see if she or he can figure out what it means.

Step Words

Go from the first word to the last word by changing one letter at a time.
Each word you make in between has to be a real word.

Change CAR to BUS.	Go from RUB to DRY.	Change WET to DRY.
car	rub	wet
cat	_____	_____
bat	_____	_____
but	_____	_____
bus	_____	_____
	dry	dry

Go from PIN to SEW.	GET to your PAY.
pin	get
_____	_____
_____	_____
_____	pay
sew	

Try one or two of your own. The first word and the last have to have
the same number of letters.

Go from _____ to _____ .   Go from _____ to _____ .

_____   _____

_____   _____

_____   _____

_____   _____

Step Words

Name _____

Go from the first word to the last word by changing one letter at a time.
Each word you make in between has to be a real word.

Change CAR to BUS.

car

cat

bat

but

bus

Go from RUB to DRY.

rub

cub

cob

coy

cry

dry

Change WET to DRY.

wet

pet

pat

pay

day

dry

Go from PIN to SEW.

pin

pit

pet

set

sew

GET to your PAY.

get

pet

pat

pay

Try one or two of your own. The first word and the last have to have
the same number of letters.

Go from _____ to _____ .   Go from _____ to _____ .

_____   _____

_____   _____

_____   _____

_____   _____

_____   _____

Rambledscword

Name _____

See how many words you can make from these groups of letters. If you want to make some sentences using the words from one group, there is space at the bottom of the page.

ostp

espt

eta

crae

eard

reba

noe

eatch

owfl

esiml

Rambledscword

See how many words you can make from these groups of letters. If you want to make some sentences using the words from one group, there is space at the bottom of the page.

ostp   *post/stop/pots/spot/tops*

espt   *pest/step/pets*

eta   *tea/eat/ate*

crae   *acre/race/care*

eard   *read/dear/dare*

reba   *bear/bare*

noe   *one/eon*

eatch   *cheat/teach*

owfl   *fowl/flow/wolf*

esiml   *miles/slime/limes/smile*

Scrambleword Sentences

Name _____

Use the letters before the sentence to make words that fill in the blanks.

ist   **1.**   It was funny to see the dog _____ on _____ own tail.

eohrs   **2.**   The _____ got sand in his hooves when he ran along the _____.

aemt   **3.**   At feeding time, we threw some _____ to the lion's _____ .

Try these without clues.

4.   When we gave it a ball of string, the _____ began to _____ like a kitten.

5.   What is the _____ of the lion shaking his _____?

6.   We always put a little _____ on our _____ to make it not so sweet.

7.   I'm not a very fast runner, so I don't _____ if I win the _____ .

8.   He uses _____ instead of glue to put his pictures on the paper. Mary

usually _____ them.

Make up one sentence of your own, and give it to somebody else to figure out.

_____

_____

Scrambleword Sentences

Name _____

Use the letters before the sentence to make words that fill in the blanks.

ist   **1.** It was funny to see the dog _____*sit*_____ on _____*its*_____ own tail.

eohrs **2.** The _____*horse*_____ got sand in his hooves when he ran along the _____*shore*_____ .

aemt   **3.** At feeding time, we threw some _____*meat*_____ to the lion's _____*mate*_____ .

Try these without clues.

4. When we gave it a ball of string, the _____*cat*_____ began to _____*act*_____ like a kitten.

5. What is the _____*name*_____ of the lion shaking his _____*mane*_____ ?

6. We always put a little _____*lemon*_____ on our _____*melon*_____ to make it not so sweet.

7. I'm not a very fast runner, so I don't _____*care*_____ if I win the _____*race*_____ .

8. He uses _____*paste*_____ instead of glue to put his pictures on the paper. Mary

usually _____*tapes*_____ them.

Make up one sentence of your own, and give it to somebody else to figure out.

_____

_____

Wordswordsinwords

Name _____

Use letters in <u>POTATOES</u> to spell words that mean:

pan ___ ___ ___

highest ___ ___ ___

chew ___ ___ ___

chair ___ ___ ___ ___

fingers on your feet ___ ___ ___ ___

put dishes on the table ___ ___ ___

your animal ___ ___ ___

honk ___ ___ ___ ___

chimney dirt ___ ___ ___ ___

what you wash with ___ ___ ___ ___

Use letters in <u>SCREWDRIVER</u> to spell words that mean:

water on the grass ___ ___ ___

animal with antlers ___ ___ ___ ___

moving water ___ ___ ___ ___ ___

jump into water ___ ___ ___ ___

fat ___ ___ ___ ___

sit on a moving animal ___ ___ ___ ___ .

bright color ___ ___ ___

an unwanted plant ___ ___ ___ ___

direction the sun sets in ___ ___ ___ ___

Use letters in <u>HANDKERCHIEF</u> to spell words that mean:

holds your palm ___ ___ ___ ___

seat ___ ___ ___ ___ ___

boss Indian ___ ___ ___ ___ ___

a thing that blows air ___ ___ ___

tool for leaves ___ ___ ___ ___

flame ___ ___ ___ ___

nice ___ ___ ___ ___

Pick out a long word, or use your name or the name of your street, and see how many words you can make out of it.

Write what the words mean, and make blanks for each letter.

See if somebody else can figure out the words.

Wordswordsinwords

Name _____

Use letters in <u>POTATOES</u> to spell words that mean:

pan <u>p</u> <u>o</u> <u>t</u>

highest <u>t</u> <u>o</u> <u>p</u>

chew <u>e</u> <u>a</u> <u>t</u>

chair <u>s</u> <u>e</u> <u>a</u> <u>t</u>

fingers on your feet <u>t</u> <u>o</u> <u>e</u> <u>s</u>

put dishes on the table <u>s</u> <u>e</u> <u>t</u>

your animal <u>p</u> <u>e</u> <u>t</u>

honk <u>t</u> <u>o</u> <u>o</u> <u>t</u>

chimney dirt <u>s</u> <u>o</u> <u>o</u> <u>t</u>

what you wash with <u>s</u> <u>o</u> <u>a</u> <u>p</u>

Use letters in <u>SCREWDRIVER</u> to spell words that mean:

water on the grass <u>d</u> <u>e</u> <u>w</u>

animal with antlers <u>d</u> <u>e</u> <u>e</u> <u>r</u>

moving water <u>r</u> <u>i</u> <u>v</u> <u>e</u> <u>r</u>

jump into water <u>d</u> <u>i</u> <u>v</u> <u>e</u>

fat <u>w</u> <u>i</u> <u>d</u> <u>e</u>

sit on a moving animal <u>r</u> <u>i</u> <u>d</u> <u>e</u> .

bright color <u>r</u> <u>e</u> <u>d</u>

an unwanted plant <u>w</u> <u>e</u> <u>e</u> <u>d</u>

direction the sun sets in <u>w</u> <u>e</u> <u>s</u> <u>t</u>

Use letters in <u>HANDKERCHIEF</u> to spell words that mean:

holds your palm <u>h</u> <u>a</u> <u>n</u> <u>d</u>

seat <u>c</u> <u>h</u> <u>a</u> <u>i</u> <u>r</u>

boss Indian <u>c</u> <u>h</u> <u>i</u> <u>e</u> <u>f</u>

a thing that blows air <u>f</u> <u>a</u> <u>n</u>

tool for leaves <u>r</u> <u>a</u> <u>k</u> <u>e</u>

flame <u>f</u> <u>i</u> <u>r</u> <u>e</u>

nice <u>k</u> <u>i</u> <u>n</u> <u>d</u>

Pick out a long word, or use your name or the name of your street, and see how many words you can make out of it.

Write what the words mean, and make blanks for each letter.

See if somebody else can figure out the words.

Palindromes

Palindromes are words that are spelled the same
forwards and backwards. Words like <u>radar</u>,
<u>mom</u>, <u>toot</u>, <u>pup</u>, and <u>solos</u> are palindromes.

Think of palindromes that mean:

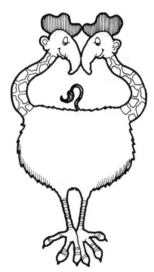

small child   _____

mid-day   _____

Miss or Mrs.   _____

flat and even   _____

joke   _____

Robert   _____

Make up some of your own.

_____   _____

_____   _____

_____   _____

_____   _____

Give them to somebody else to try.

Palindromes

Palindromes are words that are spelled the same forwards and backwards. Words like <u>radar</u>, <u>mom</u>, <u>toot</u>, <u>pup</u>, and <u>solos</u> are palindromes.

Think of palindromes that mean:

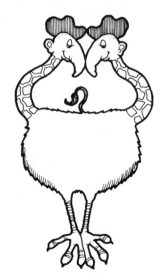

small child   _____ *tot* _____

mid-day   _____ *noon* _____

Miss or Mrs.   _____ *madam* _____

flat and even   _____ *level* _____

joke   _____ *gag* _____

Robert   _____ *Bob* _____

Make up some of your own.

_____   _____

_____   _____

_____   _____

_____   _____

Give them to somebody else to try.

Reverse

The word that fits in one blank is the word in
the other blank spelled backward. See if you
can write both words in these sentences.

1. The _____ got black, sticky feet

    when he walked on the_____ .

2. _____ paper was left _____
    the floor when they finished picking up.

3. We saw _____ fish in the _____ .

4. I'll take a _____ while the_____
    of cookies is in the oven.

5. Tell me, _____ , who _____
    the game?

6. Where does the _____ witch_____ ?

7. The man _____ using the _____ to cut the wood.

8. If you _____ one of your _____ , he won't be
    your friend any longer.

Try making up some sentences of your own and giving them to other people to try.

Reverse

Name _____

The word that fits in one blank is the word in the other blank spelled backward. See if you can write both words in these sentences.

1. The _____*rat*_____ got black, sticky feet

   when he walked on the_____*tar*_____ .

2. _____*No*_____ paper was left _____*on*_____
   the floor when they finished picking up.

3. We saw _____*ten*_____ fish in the _____*net*_____ .

4. I'll take a _____*nap*_____ while the_____*pan*_____
   of cookies is in the oven.

5. Tell me, _____*now*_____ , who _____*won*_____
   the game?

6. Where does the _____*evil*_____ witch_____*live*_____ ?

7. The man _____*was*_____ using the _____*saw*_____ to cut the wood.

8. If you _____*slap*_____ one of your _____*pals*_____ , he won't be
   your friend any longer.

Try making up some sentences of your own and giving them to other people to try.

Scrambled Sentences

Name _____

Put the words in alphabetical order to make sentences. See what they spell out.

tame
turtles
traps
Tabatha's
trembling
tiger
tall
tawny

_____
_____
_____
_____

_____
_____
_____
_____

Seely
soup
soggy
soft
sips
Sally
sharply

Many
mermaids
Mabel
merciless
massage
makes
Martians

_____
_____
_____
_____

_____
_____
_____
_____
_____

turtles
yesterday
see
Abigail
did
not
April
Albert
tough
Alonzo
and
thirty
yawn

Scrambled Sentences

Name _____

Put the words in alphabetical order to make sentences. See what they spell out.

tame
turtles
traps
Tabatha's
trembling
tiger
tall
tawny

Tabatha's tall, tame,
_____
tawny tiger traps
_____
trembling turtles.
_____
_____

Sally Seely sharply sips soft, soggy
_____
soup.
_____
_____
_____

Seely
soup
soggy
soft
sips
Sally
sharply

Many
mermaids
Mabel
merciless
massage
makes
Martians

Mabel makes many Martians massage
_____
merciless mermaids.
_____
_____
_____

Abigail, Albert, Alonzo,
_____
and April did not see
_____
thirty tough turtles
_____
yawn yesterday.
_____
_____
_____

turtles
yesterday
see
Abigail
did
not
April
Albert
tough
Alonzo
and
thirty
yawn

Classified Ads

Name _____

The classified ads in your newspaper are in alphabetical order so you can more easily find what you want.

All the cars are listed in one place, and in alphabetical order.

Cut these ads out and arrange them as they should be in the paper.

---

820   Automobiles

Mercedes Benz '69 280SE A-T, P-B, P-S, Elec. sunroof AM FM radio $5500. 591-4094.

Mercedes '60, 220B Runs Good! $800 366-9085 eves.

Mustang '65 3-speed 289 $350 366-2759 aft. 5

Caprice '74 Classic. Air, P/S, P/B, 8,000 mi. As new. $4,290 or take over pmts. 493-5885.

DODGE DART '67
Low maintenance. 22 Mi per gal. $450. 593-3592.

Dodge '72 Polara 4 Dr. Air, vinyl top, p/s, like new. $1795/offer. 948-1896.

Dodge '71, 10 Pass Sta. Wagon. Low mileage. $2100. 854-6777

BMW
H & E CAR SALES
275 Alma, Palo Alto, 324-4488

BMW 2002 '69. Red. Sunroof. New Michelins X, new Konis. $2700/offer. 854-5555.

BMW '71 2800 CS Cpe. Slvr., blue lthr., Snrf., A-T, P-S, Air, stereo, 37,000 mi. 368-6537.

Buick '66. Exc. run. cond. New tires. Clean. $400/ofr. 941-6224/493-2662 ask for Bob Clark.

DATSUN & FIAT
NEW & USED
BUY OR LEASE FOR LESS at
Dragonetti Motors
2727 El Camino
SAN MATEO
2 blks. no. of Hillsdale
Open Sun. & Eves. 'til 9
349-4455

Plymouth '49. Deluxe classic Rebuilt engine. Good condition. Best offer. 961-3431, am's.

AUDI FOX '74
2 Dr., auto, air, stereo tape, 3000 mi. Must sell. 948-2841, 493-4000 x3776.

AUDI '74 100LS 4 Dr. Automatic, Metallic blue, brand new. Save $1500 on new priced cars. #8141123451. CARLSEN PORSCHE/AUDI 1730 Embarcadero, Rd., P.A. 328-1650

ECONOMY CARS
Choose from 40 pre-owned Toyotas, Datsuns, VW's, Vegas, Pintos, etc., etc. BEST of warranties. EASY financing. Trade-ins WELCOME at THOMPSON TOYOTA, Bayshore & Whipple, Redwood City.

Dodge Charger '69, 2 dr. hardtop, 86,000 mi., A/T, gd. cond. $1025. Call 592-3302.

DODGE CENTER
640 Veterans Blvd., R.C. 365-6000
RENTALS, SALES, LEASING
Dodge Dart Swinger '70. "340" V8, p/s, a/t, a/c, scoops. $1600. 364-2402; 366-5657.

Olds. '64, Super 88, 4 dr. sedan, PS, PB, air, $250. 366-7404

OPEL Kadett '69. 4 spd., Two new Radials, $800/offer. Phone 322-2891.

OPEL KADETT '66
As is. $200. 322-7647

CHEV. '73 Vega Wagon, 4 speed, Lic. # 458 HUU. A must see. Only 16,000 miles. Carl R. Carlsen VW, 1766 E. Embarcadero Rd., P.A. 328-7100.

Chev. '73, Impala custom cpe., auto. trans., P/S, P/front disc brakes, air, AM/FM, radio, P/windows, read de-fog, 28,700 mi., beautiful buy. $3000. 366-2216.

Honda Civic '74, hatchback, brown, radio, whitewalls, 15,000 mi., $2200, 592-5585.

Jensen Healey '73. 10,000 miles. $4850. Day or night, 494-6774. Days, 967-2474.

LET'S SWAP
Used car dealer will take anything of value in trade, and help finance any remaining balance. 961-4141.

Lincoln Mark III '71. Low mi., white leather seats, AM stereo radio, tape deck, cruise control. All extras. Black exterior. Exc. cond. Reasonable. Pri. Party. 592-8511.

Buick '64, Wildcat Good Cond! $700. 366-9085 eve.

BUICK '68 Skylark sta. wagon, loaded, sharp, $1195 (VXT-697). Pay '75 lic. fees, take over pmts. NEUFELD MOTORS, 100 Main St., Redwood City; 364-0106.

Cadillac '71 Cpe. deVille. Must sell. Loaded with extra equipment. Phone 364-5059.

Ford '72 Torino sta. wag. Air, PB, PS. Exc. cond. $2500 or best offer. 851-1235.

Ford '72 Torino, Sports, P-S, P-B, Air, wide tires. Excel. cond. 1 owner. $2400. 591-5410 days, 365-0799 aft. 6

Ford '73, Squire Wagon, Brougham interior, air, beaut., cond. $3395. 365-5162.

DUSTER '73 Slanted 6, Autom., air, a1 cond. $2800. Days, 348-5411 ext. 35, eve. 364-2360.

Falcon '68 Wag. R-H, P-S, V-8, A-T. Good Cond! Asking $650. 364-0359

Fiat '57, 1100 Wag., 4 cyl. Newly reblt. eng., nds. some work. $750. Must sell. 364-4080

Fiat 600-D '62. Perfect cond. inside & out. Cust. paint. Must sell. Offer. 321-0155.

CHRYSLER 300, 1968, 4 Dr. Ht. A/C. All Extras. Ex. cond. $795. Call 964-5132.

Chrysler New Yorker '73, 4-dr., trlr. package, A/T, A/C, all pwr., orig. owner, priced to sell $3250, 325-1428.

Comet '65 V8. Rebuilt eng. Good condition. PS, PB, R&H. $750. 326-6742 eves.

GREMLIN '74, low mi., auto., loaded with extras, $2795 (234-LCQ). Pay '75 lic. fees, take over pmts. NEUFELD MOTORS, 100 Main St., Redwood City; 364-0106.

HERTZ
IS SELLING
'74 LOW MILEAGE
RECONDITIONED CARS
FOR INFO CALL 877-3737

Hillman, '50, Conv. sedan. Good cond. Orig. wide white wall tires. $1000/offer. 329-1050.

CAPRI 1972 V6. Excellent condition. Family now too large. $2,400. Call 324-0249.

Chevy Malibu '72, exc. cond., 45,000 mi., P/S, A/C, pwr. disc. brks. new radials & shocks, $2095. 968-3334.

Chevy '63 Impala, good cond., needs rear window, $250. 364-4222

Chevy '72 Concours Wagon, 9 Pass, V8, A/T, Power & Air, $1800. 969-2500 weekdays.

FIAT '69 124 COUPE
5 speed, 57k miles. $1250. Phone 328-7753

Fiat '72 124 Sport Spider conv., 5 spd., 28,000 mi., new steel belt tires, hiway 34 mpg. ex. cond. $2950. 854-5477.

FIAT '74 128 2 dr. Red. Exc. cond. $2550. 326-3295; Call any time.

Fiat 850, Roadster, '71, exc. mech. cond., $1065. 369-4811 or 364-0698.

Cut the classified ads for one product in your newspaper apart, and see if a friend can put them back in order.

Telephone Book

Name _____

Cut up these slips of paper with people's names on them, and put them in the telephone book where the names are found.

Norris	Miller
Briggs	Wood
Sullivan	Coleman
Walker	Thomas
Hill	Fisher
Alexander	Lewis
Hernandez	Wong
Williams	Reed
Dunbar	Gonzalez

Cut out some blank slips of paper the same size as these.

On the slips, write out the entire names of people in your phone book—names like Olive R. Goodman or Jerome Malaphronte.

See how quickly somebody else can put them in the telephone book where they belong.

Telephone Book

Name _____

Cut up these slips of paper with people's names
on them, and put them in the telephone book
where the names are found.

Norris	Miller
Briggs	Wood
Sullivan	Coleman
Walker	Thomas
Hill	Fisher
Alexander	Lewis
Hernandez	Wong
Williams	Reed
Dunbar	Gonzalez

Cut out some blank slips of paper the same size as these.

On the slips, write out the entire names of people in your phone book—names like
Olive R. Goodman or Jerome Malaphronte.

See how quickly somebody else can put them in the telephone book where they belong.

Homonames

Write names that go with these words.

Christmas song — _____*Carol*_____

male cat — _____

big truck — _____

blue bird — _____

spot over an I — _____

happiness _____

red flower — _____

hamburger — _____

pour full — _____

myself-myself — _____

What name is a . . .

little round thing on a bush? _____

thing you talk into to make a tape? _____

thing that lifts a car? _____

place you play basketball? _____

Pick the names of some people in your class. Write out what they mean, and see if somebody else can figure out who you mean.

47

Homonames

Write names that go with these words.

Christmas song — *Carol*

male cat — *Tom*

big truck — *Mac*

blue bird — *Jay*

spot over an I — *Dot*

happiness — *Joy*

red flower — *Rose*

hamburger — *Patty*

pour full — *Phil*

myself-myself — *Mimi*

What name is a . . .

little round thing on a bush? *Barry*

thing you talk into to make a tape? *Mike*

thing that lifts a car? *Jack*

place you play basketball? *Jim*

Pick the names of some people in your class. Write out what they mean, and see if somebody else can figure out who you mean.

The Name Sounds the Same   Name _____

Fill in the blanks with two words that sound the same but are spelled differently.

1. The black and white _____ on the _____ looked like a face.
                             fur   rabbit

2. The boy turned _____ when he saw the crabs in the _____ .
                        white   bucket

3. The captain picked up his binoculars to _____ over the _____
    for a submarine.   look   ocean

4. The poor girl was _____ on her way without a _____ .
                         made to go   penny

5. When the wind blew, you could _____ through the trees at the
                                       look

    mountain _____ .
                 top

6. It was only _____ to give each student bus _____ to and from school.
                    right   money

7. The doctor _*knows*_ when your _*nose*_ isn't right.
                 is sure   sniffer

8. Nobody _____ the big, _____ sign that said we shouldn't fish here.
              understood the   bright colored
              words on

Write one of your own. Think of two words that are spelled differently but sound the same.

_____   _____

Use them in a sentence, leaving them blank and writing a meaning underneath.

_____

_____

The Name Sounds the Same

Name _____

Fill in the blanks with two words that sound the same but are spelled differently.

1. The black and white ___*hair*___ on the ___*hare*___ looked like a face.
              fur   rabbit

2. The boy turned ___*pale*___ when he saw the crabs in the ___*pail*___ .
           white   bucket

3. The captain picked up his binoculars to ___*see*___ over the ___*sea*___
                    look   ocean
    for a submarine.

4. The poor girl was ___*sent*___ on her way without a ___*cent*___ .
           made to go   penny

5. When the wind blew, you could ___*peek*___ through the trees at the
                  look

    mountain ___*peak*___ .
          top

6. It was only ___*fair*___ to give each student bus ___*fare*___ to and from school.
          right   money

7. The doctor *knows* when your *nose* isn't right.
          is sure   sniffer

8. Nobody ___*read*___ the big, ___*red*___ sign that said we shouldn't fish here.
       understood the   bright colored
       words on

Write one of your own. Think of two words that are spelled differently but sound the same.

_____   _____

Use them in a sentence, leaving them blank and writing a meaning underneath.

_____

_____

Antonyms

One word in each sentence below is wrong.
Cross it out and write its antonym above it.

1. The man went on a diet because he was so thin.

2. You make an out if the fielder misses the fly ball.

3. Your teacher gets mad if you remember your homework.

4. John was so sad he laughed.

5. Leaves fall from the trees in the spring.

6. It is much easier to fly a kite when you add a heavy tail.

7. When the sky is blue, you know that it's going to rain.

Make up three of your own.

Antonyms

Name _____

One word in each sentence below is wrong.
Cross it out and write its antonym above it.

1. The man went on a diet because he was so ~~thin~~.
   fat

2. You make an out if the fielder ~~misses~~ the fly ball.
   catches

3. Your teacher gets mad if you ~~remember~~ your
   homework. *forget*

4. John was so ~~sad~~ he laughed.
   happy (or "so sad he cried".)

5. Leaves fall from the trees in the ~~spring~~.
   fall/autumn

6. It is much easier to fly a kite when you add a ~~heavy~~ tail.
   light

7. When the sky is ~~blue~~, you know that it's going to rain.
   gray/dark/cloudy

*These answers are just suggestions. Other answers can be
just as correct.*

Make up three of your own.

Alliteration

Name _____

Write sentences in which most of the words start with the same sound.

Here are a few we did:

Sally saw seven silly snakes sing sweetly.

Tall Tom tumbled to the top of the tree.

Mighty Mouse merrily munched monster meat.

_____

_____

_____

_____

_____

_____

_____

_____

Alliteration

Name _____

Write sentences in which most of the words start with the same sound.

Here are a few we did:

Sally saw seven silly snakes sing sweetly.

Tall Tom tumbled to the top of the tree.

Mighty Mouse merrily munched monster meat.

_____

_____

_____

_____

_____

_____

_____

_____

Kennings

People in very old England put words together to make what are called kennings. A whale was "a proud sea-thrasher," ships were called "sea-steeds," and a man's sword might be called his "dragon-destroyer."

Can you figure out these modern-day kennings?

1. gasoline gulper _____ *car* _____

2. darkness destroyer _____

3. sleep stopper _____

4. plastic song-singer _____

5. finger talk-tapper _____

6. sun smudge _____

7. tiny lead-leaver _____

8. word-eater _____

9. horsehide bat-bait _____

10. spinning water-spitter _____

11. smouldering fire-stick _____

Make up a few for somebody else to figure out.

_____   _____

_____   _____

_____   _____

_____   _____

Kennings

People in very old England put words together to make what are called kennings. A whale was "a proud sea-thrasher," ships were called "sea-steeds," and a man's sword might be called his "dragon-destroyer."

Can you figure out these modern-day kennings?

1. gasoline gulper _____ *car* _____
2. darkness destroyer _____ *sun/light* _____
3. sleep stopper _____ *alarm clock* _____
4. plastic song-singer _____ *record* _____
5. finger talk-tapper _____ *typewriter/teletype* _____
6. sun smudge _____ *cloud/freckle* _____
7. tiny lead-leaver _____ *pencil* _____
8. word-eater _____ *eraser* _____
9. horsehide bat-bait _____ *baseball* _____
10. spinning water-spitter _____ *sprinkler* _____
11. smouldering fire-stick _____ *cigarette/pipe* _____

Make up a few for somebody else to figure out.

_____   _____

_____   _____

_____   _____

_____   _____

Draw-a-Word

Draw a word, showing what it means by the way you write it.

Here are a few:

Others for you to try: run, sun, fog, round, flat, spiral, music, fall, wide, rabbit.

Make up some of your own, too.

Draw-a-Word

Draw a word, showing what it means by the way you write it.

Here are a few:

Others for you to try: run, sun, fog, round, flat, spiral, music, fall, wide, rabbit.

Make up some of your own, too.

Draw-a-Poem

Name _____

Write a short poem or sentence about something. Then print it so that it shows what it is about. You may want to paint the background with water colors or crayons.

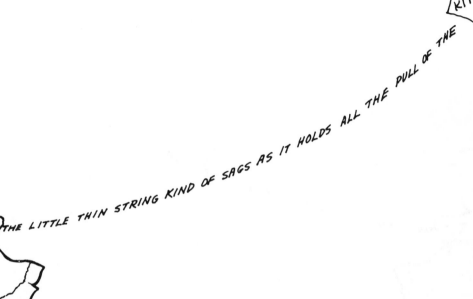

THE LITTLE THIN STRING KIND OF SAGS AS IT HOLDS ALL THE PULL OF THE KITE AND ITS TAIL

You might write about boats, water, a tree or plant, stars, sports, a color.

Your poem: _____

_____

Draw it.

Draw-a-Poem

Write a short poem or sentence about something. Then print it so that it shows what it is about.

You may want to paint the background with water colors or crayons.

THE LITTLE THIN STRING KIND OF SAGS AS IT HOLDS ALL THE PULL OF THE KITE AND ITS TAIL

You might write about boats, water, a tree or plant, stars, sports, a color.

Your poem: _____

_____

Draw it.

007 Strikes Again

Name _____

Here is a code direction. Do it.

write *your* *name* *backwards*
23 18 9 20 5 X 25 15 21 18 X 14 1 13 5 X 2 1 3 11 23 1 18 4 19

at *the* *top* *of* *the* *page*
X 1 20 X 20 8 5 X 20 15 16 X 15 6 X 20 8 5 X 16 1 7 5

This is a different kind of code. Write the sentence under the code.

THECLOUDFLOATEDTHROUGHTHESKY.

_____

thewavescrashroughlyontheshoreandslowlyglideoutagain.

_____

adaffodilopeneditspetalsandsaidhello.

_____

assoonasyoubakethecakeeatit.

_____

Write a sentence of your own in one of these codes, or in a code you make up yourself. Then give it to somebody you want to figure it out.

_____

_____

007 Strikes Again

Name _____

Here is a code direction. Do it.

23 18 9 20 5 X 25 15 21 18 X 14 1 13 5 X 2 1 3 11 23 1 18 4 19
write ... *your* ... *name* ... *backwards*

X 1 20 X 20 8 5 X 20 15 16 X 15 6 X 20 8 5 X 16 1 7 5
at ... *the* ... *top* ... *of* ... *the* ... *page*

This is a different kind of code. Write the sentence under the code.

THECLOUDFLOATEDTHROUGHTHESKY.

> *The cloud floated through the sky.*
_____

thewavescrashroughlyontheshoreandslowlyglideoutagain.

> *The waves crash roughly on the shore and slowly glide out again.*
_____

adaffodilopeneditspetalsandsaidhello.

> *A daffodil opened its petals and said hello.*
_____

assoonasyoubakethecakeeatit.

> *As soon as you bake the cake, eat it.*
_____

Write a sentence of your own in one of these codes, or in a code you make up yourself. Then give it to somebody you want to figure it out.

_____

_____

What Are They?

Name _____

A. _____

B. _____

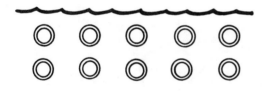

C. _____

D. _____

Make up at least one of your own.

Put it on a card with the answer on the back.

What Are They?

Name _____

A. *A caterpillar on roller skates*

B. *A swordfish taking a donut*

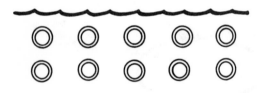

C. *A ship's portholes, as seen by a fish*

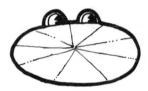

D. *A frog looking out from behind a lily pad*

Make up at least one of your own.

Put it on a card with the answer on the back.

Letter-Word

Name _____

One answer is a letter or letters; the other is a word.

_U_	_you_	Yourself
_J_	_____	bluebird
_EZ_	_easy_	simple
_____	_____	Indian tent
_____	_____	all right
_____	_____	stinging insect
_____	_____	look
_____	_____	what for?
_____	_____	a small, round green vegetable
_____	_____	what you see with

Write the sentence under the letters.

1. R U OK?

   _____

2. Y did the B drink T?

   _____

3. I C TV.

   _____

4. The TP is MT.

   _____

5. KT, R U a QT?

   _____

Make up a sentence, and give it to somebody to try.

Letter-Word

Name _____

One answer is a letter or letters; the other is a word.

_U_	_you_	Yourself
_J_	_jay_	bluebird
_E z_	_easy_	simple
_TP_	_teepee_	Indian tent
_OK_	_okay_	all right
_B_	_bee_	stinging insect
_C_	_see_	look
_Y_	_why_	what for?
_P_	_pea_	a small, round green vegetable
_I_	_eye_	what you see with

Write the sentence under the letters.

1. R U OK?

    Are you OK?

2. Y did the B drink T?

    Why did the bee drink tea?

3. I C TV.

    I see TV.

4. The TP is MT.

    The teepee is empty.

5. KT, R U a QT?

    Katie, are you a cutie?

Make up a sentence, and give it to somebody to try.

License Plates

Many states let people pay extra to pick their own license plates. The plates must have at least two letters, but no more than six. Numbers can be put in place of two letters.

Here are some license plates. See if you can guess who might want them from the list underneath them. Write whose you think they might be beside them.

TREE DR _____   PET VET _____

P NUTS _____   REED IT _____

E Z WIN _____   I C WELL _____

B MINE _____   10 NIS _____

TEE P _____   A1 AN A2 _____

Pitcher, Indian, nut salesperson, card salesperson, eye doctor, animal doctor, tennis player, bookstore owner, tree surgeon, Lawrence Welk.

Make up some of your own license plates.

Give them to a friend to figure out.

License Plates

Name _____

Many states let people pay extra to pick their own license plates. The plates must have at least two letters, but no more than six. Numbers can be put in place of two letters.

Here are some license plates. See if you can guess who might want them from the list underneath them. Write whose you think they might be beside them.

Plate	Answer
TREE DR	*tree surgeon*
P NUTS	*nut salesperson*
E Z WIN	*pitcher*
B MINE	*card salesperson*
TEE P	*Indian*

Plate	Answer
PET VET	*animal doctor*
REED IT	*bookstore owner*
I C WELL	*eye doctor*
10 NIS	*tennis player*
A1 AN A2	*Lawrence Welk*

Pitcher, Indian, nut salesperson, card salesperson, eye doctor, animal doctor, tennis player, bookstore owner, tree surgeon, Lawrence Welk.

Make up some of your own license plates.

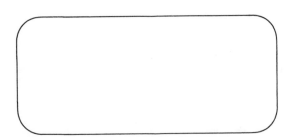

Give them to a friend to figure out.

Hangman

Hangman is a game to play with somebody else.

First you think of a word. Then you draw as many blanks as there are letters in the word.
If you thought of spaghetti, you would draw nine blanks, since there are nine letters in spaghetti.

Now, have the other person try to guess letters in the word, one at a time. For each guess that is right, you write the letter in the blank or blanks it goes in. For each wrong guess, you draw one part of the hanged man.

If the man is drawn before the other person guesses the word, you win.

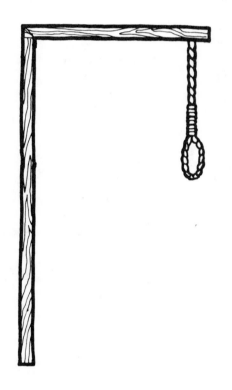

parts of the man

head

neck

body

arms

hands

legs

feet

Hangman

Hangman is a game to play with somebody else.

First you think of a word. Then you draw as many blanks as there are letters in the word.
If you thought of spaghetti, you would draw nine blanks, since there are nine letters in spaghetti.

Now, have the other person try to guess letters in the word, one at a time. For each guess that
is right, you write the letter in the blank or blanks it goes in. For each wrong guess, you draw
one part of the hanged man.

If the man is drawn before the other person guesses the word, you win.

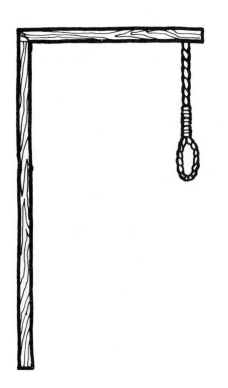

parts of the man

    head

    neck

    body

    arms

    hands

    legs

    feet